Resilience-Centered Counseling

Resilience-Centered Counseling

A Liberating Approach for Change and Wellbeing

Colin Ward, Bill Heusler, and Katherine Nordell Fort

cognella

SAN DIEGO

Bassim Hamadeh, CEO and Publisher
Amy Smith, Senior Project Editor
Jeanine Rees, Production Editor
Jess Estrella, Senior Graphic Designer
Michaleigh Moylan, Licensing Associate
Natalie Piccotti, Director of Marketing
Kassie Graves, Vice President of Editorial
Jamie Giganti, Director of Academic Publishing

Cover image copyright © 2018 iStockphoto LP/pigphoto.

Printed in the United States of America.

cognella® | ACADEMIC PUBLISHING
3970 Sorrento Valley Blvd., Ste. 500, San Diego, CA 92121

The bamboo tree, known as one of the fastest growing plants in the world, begins slowly. The roots take time to become established, as they seek connection to the surrounding grove for nourishment as well as depth to assist with stability. They grow best in pairs, and as the young trees increase their capacity for one another as well as their surroundings, they find depth. Connection in this way promotes not only rapid growth but also the ability to withstand adverse conditions. This is relational resilience: stabilized through attachment and deepened by a shared experience of belonging with community, culture, and, most importantly, one another. Withstanding adversity is not a single tree bending in the wind, nor an individual arising alone in the darkness upon falling. It is other-reliant and inter-dependent: All those that fall find support in the faith that others have in their strength to stand again ... a faith that only comes when standing together arm in arm.

—Colin Ward & Keiko Sano, 2021

Brief Contents

Detailed Contents

Preface

A Note from Bill

I have never written a preface before and in taking on this task I had to think about what could be said that would make what is about to be said something you (the reader) would find even more inviting. This became more than an afterthought, and a struggle ensued. I found myself struggling with all the things I find myself struggling with when I am stalled. As often happens, when this happens, I looked backwards and inwards and a story from another time came to mind. When I was fully engaged in another life and career, I needed an escape to depressurize from time to time. I took up fishing, tournament bass fishing to be exact. I befriended another fisherperson, Sam, whom I immediately liked. I am not sure why I was so fond of him: We did not agree on anything about anything ... politics, fishing equipment, favorite movies, TV shows, music, food, coffee, beer. You name it, and we would argue about it. People often wondered, when they would see us fishing together, which one of us was not coming back. Sam had 32 stories. I know; I numbered them. For the most part, he would tell the same stories in the same order every time we went fishing, which numbered in the hundreds of times.

On one particular morning, we were fishing on Mark Twain Lake outside of Hannibal, MO (of course). Mark Twain Lake is a flood control lake that was established by the Army Corp of Engineers in a somewhat futile attempt to control flooding on the Mississippi River. The night before, they had dropped the water level on the lake by about 20 feet. This resulted in all the debris, logs, and brush that was floating around from when they raised the water a week before to collect along the banks. We were trolling along when we came upon a shallow cut in the bank where about 30 feet of debris stood between us and a small pool of clear water at the back of the cut against the bank. I eyed that pool in anticipation, as this is the perfect place for a bass to lurk in wait of prey. I then realized that landing a fish after dragging it over all the debris was likely an impossible mission and started looking ahead for safer water along the bank. Sam stood up and tossed a plastic worm, landing it perfectly at the bank edge of the pool of water on the other side of all those logs. I looked up at Sam and in my usual sarcastic and caustic tone asked, "How are you going to get a fish out of there?!" shaking my head at the folly of his effort. Sam hooked a fish in that pool and gently slid it over the debris, one log at a time, all the way back to the boat (he had been doing this for decades). He looked over at me and said, "There you go again, always focused on the second problem."

I still have a tendency to think far ahead beyond the first problem. Maybe some of you do as well, and if you are anything like me, you may find yourself fascinated by this thing we call "psychotherapy" and "counseling." When starting out, I could not wait to learn about this model or that model, this intervention or that intervention, this epistemology or that one. I became immersed in the alphabet soup of psychotherapies (e.g., CBT, ACT, DBT, SFBT, REBT, EFT, IFS, EMDR, CCT, etc.), determined to find just the right thing to do at just the right time to turn the world of one suffering person around before moving on to the next person. Then a client would show up, and as I thumbed through the file cabinet of models to match with this person, Sam's words come back to me and I settle down, sit with this person, and just get to know them. What are they about, what are they doing, who are they, and why are they doing this? I open myself up to who this person is and what they want. Models, techniques, and interventions fall in the class of things Sam referred to as the "second problem," and it is important to get the order correct, or you might find yourself looking for safer water when what you really need is sitting there right in front of you.

This book started a few years ago with an encounter when I met Colin in the halls of Antioch University Seattle where we both were teaching in different programs: Colin in the Mental Health Counseling Program and Bill in the PsyD Program. We seemed to hit it off like brothers from a different mother. You know that feeling you get when you realize you went to different high schools together? We read the same books a hundred years ago and shared many of the same ideas, and then the humor entered the scene. Laughter became a much-needed part of every conversation. Then along came Katherine taking up residence in Colin's program with a breath of fresh air, a more optimistic view, a focused intelligence, and clear social justice values. Colin approached me just ahead of the pandemic with a question: "Do you want to write a book?" We started and as we did the world began to shut down. We had to switch gears literally overnight and shift our teaching to an online approach—a task that would normally take months in planning. We had about 2 weeks. Things stalled a bit; we were struggling with how to make some things different and unique for this work. Colin invited Katherine to consult on some ideas, and we realized that what we needed was fresh eyes, and Katherine's were there and looking and telling us what she was seeing in the work. Two became three, and we are all three the better for it. We started meeting over the ubiquitous Zoom application every Tuesday morning, and the work started to take off! This is not a new combination where counseling and psychology come together to better understand how therapy works. This trio is perhaps one of the few to collaborate so closely together, reading and revising each other's ideas, writing, editing, proposing, and developing chapters. Sometimes one would take the lead on a chapter or topic, and we always seemed to allow for and make room for each other in every aspect of this book. We hope you will find the harmony pleasing to the ear. We surely do.

A Note from Colin

Counseling is a profession that shapes our lives. It requires a willingness to hear the experience of others while acknowledging our own. Being a counselor has influenced how I view my relationships, myself, and the world around me. As much as I have grown professionally, I have been equally invited to grow personally. Maybe that is the difference when transitioning from *acting* like a counselor to actually *becoming* one. The idea that professional development is in constant motion, a weaving of previous insights with immediate and novel clinical experiences, fits with how I have considered my own growth as well as the growth of others around me. As I reflect on my career over the past 33 years, I am reminiscent on select professional benchmarks. I hope that by taking a brief look back, the path forward, as you begin or continue your professional work with others, might have footing. These are especially important in areas of troublesome soils. And so ...

Having been a special educator, I began my clinical career with the intent of helping others think more clearly, act more responsibly, and consider themselves with worth. My peers and I were armed with the tools of CBT, reality therapy, transactional analysis, and the skills of empathic listening gleaned from the works of Carl Rogers: with the belief that insight and strengthening another's ego states would lead others toward a life better lived. We were counselors and, in some regard, considered ourselves healers.

Around that time, the American Counseling Association challenged counselors to leave the four walls of our offices and address the social dynamics impacting the mental health and life quality of our clients. I became part of a field that viewed our work as a community service—to address the impact of oppression on the lived experience of our clients while also seeking ways to mitigate those same oppressive forces. The emergence of family systems and multicultural counseling theory added support to the idea that we are each uniquely shaped by intersecting identities as well as overlapping parts of a larger whole. As Martin Luther King Jr. noted, "Injustice anywhere is a threat to justice everywhere." We were also social advocates.

I witnessed the disparities of those with access to counseling services and those without. The rising cost of insurance ushered in the policies of managed medical and mental health care. Reimbursement now came with a price tag: to demonstrate that what we do makes a difference. We were accountable to the outcomes of our work, and the results consistently showed (and still do) that regardless of one's theoretical approach, if the inherent resources and strengths are utilized, if counselors show up with warmth, respect, and fidelity, and if the client and counselor perceive their relationship as trustworthy, good things happen. Understanding how best to empower the counseling relationship to empower others and the communities in which they lived became an essential feature of our professional work. We were counselors and advocates, clients were the healers, and we were becoming action researchers.

Neurobiology assisted counselors in making better sense of the stress response system and how trauma symptoms were merely efforts of the mind and body to make sense of the unexplainable. It provided a window to see people not as broken but inherently capable of restoration. The rise of somatic and strength-centered therapies reflect this emergent gaze. We began to see our role as collaborators, advocates that stand alongside others as they chart their own path. Wellness became less about applying mindfulness and self-care activities and more about being mindful in the face of adverse and stressful experiences. We are counselors, witnesses to the inherent self-healing capacity of people, communities, and systems.

These are our professional footings: an emergent lens reflecting the beauty of the human spirit and the inherent restorative abilities of people. Appreciating how individuals have been "stretched" by life's struggles allows a window into those resilient attributes necessary in one's fight for freedom and agency. If you believe that we find in others what we believe to be true for ourselves, then if you have faith in the unique and surprising resources of people as they confront the often insurmountable odds to a better life, you will find such ... together.

Our desire to write a text arose from this belief and a frustration that counselor training had become overly influenced by research of what to do rather than the research of who to become as therapists. As Bill noted, in an effort to produce results, the field became preoccupied with the second problem, emphasizing counselor expertise rather than considering the first problem: How do people recover and change, and what is needed to support these naturally occurring dynamics? If the client and not the counselor is the expert, then how can people be provided opportunities to recognize and apply their own agency? It was this shared belief in others that connected Bill,

Katherine, and myself together. We recognized that regardless of our extensive trainings, what we did had little influence on whether or not people changed. We concluded it was how we showed up with others and, in many ways, with each other. We talked about our ferocious faith in the power of self-healing and how when confronted with enormous challenges and traumas, people recover, restore, and reconnect. Our first problem as therapists—in fact, the only problem we need to be concerned about—is to how to listen without rescuing and how to appreciate life's struggle and suffering not as something that needs to be removed, replaced, or diagnosed but as the essential life experience that ushers in resilience. This text seeks to provide added footing into how counselors can conceptualize their work with clients as well as their own professional development, from a resilience-centered foundation.

You are part of a field that will shape you as much as you as you seek to shape it. It is our hope that in your service to our professional ideals—respect, responsibility, and humility—you will allow space for grace when you fall short. Bill, Katherine, and I talked a lot about this; how each of us are an unfolding, a process nurtured by the light of our better selves and influenced by recognizing this in one another.

To paraphrase Fredrick Lenz, a master of art is someone who's been mastered by the art ... where the teacher and student are indistinguishable from one another. We hope you find this text as a continuing conversation toward the art of your own professional becoming.

A Note from Katherine

To coauthor a book on resilience during a global pandemic has been such a gift, and I am so grateful to Colin and Bill for asking me to join them in this adventure. During this process, our conversations added just the right amount of levity, groundedness, and self-reflection needed to keep on trudging through a pretty challenging time. Yet it was not until the end of this process that I really stopped to realize just how "meta" this experience has been: tapping into relational resilience practices with one another, learning about each other's lived experiences and world views in order to find the resilience necessary to then think more deeply about resilience itself, and then writing about it. In a way, the challenges of the pandemic helped us to concretely conceptualize just what we had each been thinking about and noticing in our years of work as helping professionals. True healing happens in partnership and in community. It is bidirectional, and when approached with humility, transparency, curiosity, and compassion—for both ourselves and our clients—we can really get to some incredible outcomes.

Just today, one of my supervisees asked, "What is it, do you think, that keeps people going in the face of adversity?" Before answering, I asked if a client had asked her this question—was that why it was coming up? Her client had indeed asked this question, and my supervisee had provided her authentic answer. It was a beautiful answer, and it was very true to my supervisee: her framework and her outlook on life. As we talked about that experience, what it was like for her to answer her client so authentically with what my supervisee worried may have been too transparent or too self-disclosing, we also discussed how useful it might be to have the client answer this for herself. Of course, this is what counseling textbooks tell you to do: to turn the "self-disclosing" type question back to the client and ask, "Well, what do you think?" But often in practice, we miss the true opportunity in holding this direction of focus. Yes, the client may be able to hear themselves in a new way, and yes, the focus can better stay on the client, but we also must remember that we, too, have a chance to learn from our client in moments such as this: their worldview, their beliefs, what is meaningful to them.

The act of personal authenticity in a moment like this, I believe, also holds so much potential. We, together, get to know one another as humans and grow in that space. That awareness and growth, in an atmosphere of nonjudgment and deep listening, is sacred. As counselors, we are so privileged to hold this space, a space that those in pain need and deserve, and as human beings ourselves, this connection is also deeply meaningful to our own existence. This capacity for change-making that we hold as advocates as well as the constant learning that we gain in our "seat" in the room are equally important outcomes in our work. Counseling is relational, and therefore, it is bidirectional. Being "Oz" behind the curtain, the expert, or the sage on the stage only leads to harm in the long run. Imbalances of power are maintained, and systems of oppression go unchanged. When we approach our work relationally, authentically, and with humility, we move in the direction of equity and justice. To me, that is where real resilience lies—together. So, I ask you first: What is it, do you think, that keeps people going in the face of adversity? Your answer says so much about you, your lived experiences, your culture, your beliefs. Those are beautiful and unique pieces that make you who you are. As humans, we likely do not all share or even agree on the same answer, and that is ok. In fact, it is great! It is our *collection* of answers to such questions and more so the process of speaking and listening to them together that points toward a common humanity. In that moment of hearing one another, we lift each other up. We learn. We grow. And in the end, that is my answer. I think that as living beings, we long to grow and to be truly seen by others for who we are—most especially in the face of adversity.

Introduction

To varying degrees, people are confronted with challenges and emotional reactions that can quickly lead to despair and isolation if they forget that the weight of each step is more about the climb than themselves (the climber). As mental health professionals, an overemphasis on pathology, deficits, disorders, and personality limits the breadth and depth of our work as well as denies clients the invitation into their very best. This is the essence of resilient living and the bridge to healing and renewal. Most counseling theory books highlight an overview to theories and approaches with little attention to what actually works in counseling. *Resilience-Centered Counseling* highlights the current intersection of neurobiology and resilience with integrated relevant counseling theory to how clinicians can collaboratively assist others with mapping out pathways needed to "bounce back" from adverse life circumstances.

The purpose of this book is to provide mental health professionals, counselor educators, and supervisors with a therapeutic approach accentuating an individual's capacity for change and regeneration. Grounded in the principles of postmodernism, humanism, feminism, and neurobiology, with an emphasis on evidence-informed practices, each chapter seeks to engage the reader in a new way of understanding the clinical encounter, an encounter grounded in the undeniable recognition that people are far more than the challenges faced, that change is inevitable given the right conditions, and that counseling is a collaborative invitation to one's "better self" in resistance to anxious and worrisome thoughts. In the tradition of brief therapy approaches, *Resilience-Centered Counseling* is a reimagining of how clinicians can work efficiently and pragmatically. It guides the reader with how to adopt a stance and skill set toward transforming client struggles into something different: different in mindset, different in the relationships one has with others, different in the relationship with one's self, and different in how therapeutic moments present themselves in and out of the counseling office.

Part I of the text begins with a chapter exploring how the current training and supervision of mental health professionals emphasize the skills and knowledge of the counselor and how those qualities embodied by clients and families are often found to be insignificant to treatment outcomes. The second chapter notes the intellectual structures of consciousness and empiricism that view the role of counselors as healers in the lives of their clients. The limitations of this traditional stance usher in Chapter 3 and the paradigm of self-healing. This chapter centers on the inherent healing capacity of people and how the counseling relationship can provide space for clients to heal and transform. Chapters 4–8 elicit further understanding of self-healing in reference to those theoretical frames that make real differences in the lives of people. This includes the dynamics of interdependency (Chapter 4), where understanding the intersecting contextual experiences of others provides an appreciation to the whole of an individual and not just a dissection of parts; second order change (Chapter 5), where individual growth occurs within meaningful relationships; trauma and resilience (Chapter 6), where witnessing the experience of another's story rather than the story itself invites opportunities for self-soothing, imagination, and a broader sense of who people wish to become; postmodernism (Chapter 7), where all perspectives are layered in truth and client self-narratives are broadened to include options for self-determined change; and, finally, feminism and resilience

(Chapter 8), where by supporting the internal power of clients, the contextual terrains of one's past, present, and future can unfold truths for a truer self.

Part II of the book highlights how counselors can utilize the theoretical gaze of self-healing as referenced in Part I to open space for resilient clinical narratives and action. Chapter 9 decolonizes the definition of "resilience" and highlights how resilience-centered relationships can work to transform client suffering into strengths, despair into hope, and loneliness into a greater sense of connection. Infusing a social justice stance to these resilience-centered counseling relationships is the focus of Chapter 10, where the myth of meritocracy is replaced with self-determination, equity, and relational agency. Chapters 11–13 highlight those clinical features essential to resilience-centered counseling. Surfing (Chapter 11) assist others with embracing the uncomfortable, as people, families, and communities come to terms with overwhelming events. Wonderment (Chapter 12) is the commitment to experience others for the first time every time, with ferocious curiosity and unconditional acceptance. Chapter 13 maps out how counselors can assist others with remembering the better parts of themselves forgotten over time, clouded by adversity, and hidden by fear and shame. Finally, Chapter 14 provides a guide to assist therapists in learning the intent, language, and stance of resilience-centered counseling.

Counselor training is more than just the acquisition of knowledge and skills. It requires capacity to hold therapeutic space with an emphasis on understanding, appreciating, and acknowledging the inherent strengths and resources of others as they struggle toward better versions of themselves in the face of dissonant life circumstances and events. It is not the absence of solid training in psychodiagnosis and empirical approaches to clinical treatment, but a style of being with others that is not distracted by it. This is a style that recognizes the essential truth that only people can change themselves. Incorporating interactive activities, case examples, and interview guides to assist in the application of *Resilience-Centered Counseling*, each chapter engages the reader to reconsider their assumptions in both their counseling work with others as well as with themselves. By seeing people as resilient, capable, and strong, the need for clinicians to treat and intervene is replaced with an unwavering belief that by creating collaborative and resilience-centered counseling relationships, people are provided the atmosphere to heal, connect, and transform themselves into their preferred versions.

Finally, this book is to be experienced as much as it is to be read. In the same way a resilience-centered approach to counseling offers others opportunities to reflect in counterintuitive ways, the learning activities accompanying the text provide the same with the reader. By presenting a new paradigm of brief therapy, the emphasis on learning and the translation of theory to clinical practice is what makes this text both unique and relevant. Since counseling has little to do with helping others be happy and everything to do with helping them become stronger, this book is designed for those counselors and therapists seeking to join their clientele in a liberation from the weight of depression, the fatigue of anxiety, the devastations of trauma, and the chains of deprecating self-narratives and fears. It is our hope that following the experience that readers have with this book, they will begin to have therapeutic moments with others that incite the energy needed to open space for the possible and collaboratively access the resources needed for change and well-being—for both themselves and others.

PART I

A RESILIENT THEORETICAL GAZE

Counselor as Healer

We know what we are, but know not what we may be.

—William Shakespeare

Every year graduate students express concern that faculty spend too much time and attention talking about the importance of the quality of the counseling relationship and do not focus enough on interventions and techniques. Like most novice clinicians, they want to "do something," to take an action that might demonstrate their benevolence by relieving the pain of others. This is their effort to secure a helping role, one that can make others feel better. There is a lot of pressure in graduate training; students are asked to demonstrate competence in accordance with national professional standards, which reflect the rise of empirically supported treatments emphasizing the importance of complying with manualized treatment protocols. Within this lie a vast array of counseling theories, a toolbox of ideas explaining the unexplainable, attached to actions directing people to change in predetermined ways. It is no wonder that clinicians approach the counseling relationship with a belief that they have, or should have, the hidden key to help the wounded heal. With these pressures and expectations, many helping professionals give themselves and their interventions the majority of credit for client change, even though research shows that the most important contributors to clinical outcomes are clients themselves and the cohesion, or alliance, they experience within the counseling relationship (Elliot et al., 2019; Bohart & Tallman, 2010; Lambert, 1992). This chapter explores how the training and supervision of mental health professionals have emphasized the skills and knowledge of the counselor to the point where the resilient qualities of those they serve are often ignored. In a profession focused on understanding the texture of human experience, we have at times forgotten the purpose. There is an old saying that once you find yourself in the middle of a swamp, it is hard to remember why you entered in the first place. Is our purpose to relieve the pain of others or is it to assist in such a way that others hold, tolerate, and transform their pain themselves? In a profession focused on understanding the texture of human experience, we have at times forgotten the reason why we ventured into the uncharted waters of others. This chapter sets the stage in remembering that the way through is best navigated by the client, working in a shared journey alongside the counselor. In the end, it is the client and the quality of the therapeutic relationship that heals … always.

Theory driven models still shape the essential core knowledge that counseling students wrestle within graduate school, yet there is little or no discernable difference between the vast number of theoretical approaches in psychotherapy with regard to client outcomes or presenting concerns (Wampold, 2001). In fact, the singular predictor to positive counseling outcomes, regardless of theoretical orientation, are relational dynamics (Norcross & Lambert, 2019; Norcross, 2011; Hubble et al., 2004; Duncan et al., 2010). These dynamics are clearly under the influence of the therapist from the very start. As Lambert (1992) pointed out in his review of counseling outcomes, the counseling relationship can empower and motivate people in the process of change and account for up to 17% of the total variance to outcome—far exceeding that which techniques or theoretical models can explain. Moreover, differences in the clinician's approach to this relationship have been shown to have a greater impact on counseling outcomes than the use of any theoretical techniques. In a study conducted by Norcross (2002), qualities of empathy and collaboration were reported to be demonstrably effective, while conditions of positive regard, congruence, and management of countertransference were promising and probably effective. Unfortunately, the counseling relationship is *the* tool that new counselors most struggle to accentuate. Likely, this difficulty reflects how novice counselors are so concerned with "getting it right" and connecting all the dots from theory to intervention that they are blind to the dynamics in the room. At the core, they are still too focused on themselves.

Evidence suggests that client strengths and circumstances greatly affect the overall outcome of counseling (Cuijpers et al., 2012). Lambert (1992) estimate that 40% of the total variance associated with the outcomes of psychotherapy is ascribed to clients and events that occur between counseling sessions. The question for counselors today is not just what works in counseling but also what works on the path of a client empowering themselves in the face of adversity. This singular emphasis on client context is often lost when counselors merely "apply" therapeutic models. When therapists are trained with the idea that they can heal others, what is forgotten is how others have the capacity to heal themselves. A client once expressed to me (Colin) toward the end of our work together how they initially hoped I might relieve them of their pain and hurt. They expressed how their initial disappointment in my unwillingness to prescribe solutions was replaced with astonishment that "you genuinely believed I could work through my struggles even when I (and others) doubted this." Insight and change become less about the expertise of counselors and the theoretical formulations informing their actions, and more about the dispositions that counselors utilize to promote therapeutic relationships. In other words, how can counselors show up in a way that acknowledges the inherent resilient qualities of individuals and families as well as their capacity to withstand and thrive in the very face of life's challenges? The following is a brief exploration of two essential dynamics in reference to this question: the counseling relationship and empathy.

The Counseling Relationship

The relationships that surround us are considered our support system. The fabric of attachments formed in infancy and childhood as we grow and develop becomes a very large part of our reality. Throughout our careers, we have found that not a single client, couple, or family has noted in their experience of psychotherapy one single intervention or technique that made the most difference in their experience of counseling. Regardless of our approach at the time (and over the years this has taken some twists and turns), the overwhelming message concerning what mattered most was the relationship. "We believed you cared about us," one family wrote. "It seemed you were interested in our well-being and had our back," "I felt there was nothing I couldn't talk with you about," or "I knew that I could tell you anything in a space without judgment" are some examples of statements given by clients. These words might sound familiar in your own work with others. It was not so much the depth of knowledge we had about the science of our field but how others experienced us: as caring helpers, as humans in partnership with them as they faced life's challenges. This is not to say our training experiences were not important; they just were not viewed, as noted in the research by our clients, as central in their efforts toward finding understanding and creating change.

Additionally, when we examined the reasons why our clients came to counseling, among other things, we have consistently found that our clients have been in need of a healthy support system. This is evidenced by the fact that there are several models of counseling that focus almost exclusively on building a client's relationship capacity (e.g., Glasser's reality therapy [1975] or Teyber's interpersonal process therapy [2010]). Furthermore, nearly all models and theories see this critical baseline and assert that one must first establish a therapeutic relationship in order to do therapy in the first place. We would suggest that over the past 150 years, psychotherapists have focused significant energy and attention on helping people find ways to tolerate the distress of difficult relationships; enhance abilities to manage and improve relationships; identify and mitigate unhealthy or troubling relationships; deconstruct and reconstruct relationships with family, society, and environment; and heal the relationship with the self. These constant themes highlight the important role of the therapeutic relationship as a baseline. Reminiscent of Bowlby's (1977) work on attachment, the counselor seeks to provide a "secure base" to hold the corrective emotional experience for insecurely attached clients and a container for the anxiety-provoking work of therapy. By providing an honest and genuine presence with unconditional acceptance, the counselor allows others an opportunity to tolerate this in themselves. Shore (2012) believed that a hallmark of resilience is the ability to self-regulate in the face of interpersonal distress—providing the space needed to turn toward collaborative rather than defensive reactions. For counselors, it is a refrain from managing an experience of another's distress by soothing, comforting, reassuring, or seeking to remove the distress of another through an intervention or problem solving. To do so is to give the impression that clients are unable to do such for themselves and can promote discouragement and maintain an inner experience of being oppressed as well as reenacting, perpetuating, or creating unhealthy dependencies.

Respecting clients means receiving them with an open attitude toward emotions, thoughts, and sensations where negative emotions and challenges are viewed as an inevitable part of the human experience: reflective of developmental changes in identity and social roles, daily life stressors, and striving to organize a life built around meaningful experiences, goals, and values. This ability to "hold space" for another is an attunement to the dissonance that exists when two or more conflicting experiences coexist. This dissonance is a natural phenomenon in the human relational experience, as we each walk our own path and have our own experiences that make up our lived identities. Thus, deeply listening to the person across from us without judgment and without bringing in our own agenda requires counselors to hold a reverent space for another's experience while also holding on to their own. Holding space for others in this way, as noted by Eve Lipchik (2011), allows people to change themselves as opposed to being changed by counselors.

Bowen's (1978) idea of differentiation sought to address this therapeutic dynamic. He argued that personal growth is contingent on a self-reflective process to modulate emotionality in the face of tension or conflict. Likewise, Mezirow (1994) contended that personal meaning is created when individuals face unfamiliar situations within the secure attachment of counseling relationships, as demonstrated by a counselor's expression of empathy, acceptance, and unconditional positive regard in response to client distress, fear, and apprehension. In contrast to many approaches of counseling, which seek to reduce or eliminate client discomfort, holding secure space with others is an empathic encounter that seeks to shift how people describe themselves in relationship to the problems they wish resolved. From a resilience perspective, it is not the removal of an "irrational" thought, an inappropriate behavior, or even how best to live with a personal deficit, but the addition of something else: meaning, possibility, hope, strength, and resilience. We believe that this aids clients in creating space for their lived experiences; past, present, and future. It also honors a way of being with themselves and others that is aligned with their deepest values instead of being narrowly focused on achieving happiness.

Miller (2001) imagined this as a counselor acting as a "curious conversationalist" (p. 80), intent on understanding how the inner dissonance of others is an expression of meaning (e.g., compromised values, unmet needs or expectations). In contrast to a knowing "expert," the counselor embodies a stance, as described by Anderson and Goolishian (1992), of *not* knowing. They wrote that this is represented by a

> general attitude or stance in which the therapist's actions communicate an abundant, genuine curiosity. That is, the therapist's actions and attitudes express a need to know more about what has been said, rather than convey preconceived opinions and expectations about the client, the problem, or what must be changed. The therapist, therefore, positions himself or herself in such a way as always to be in a state of "being informed" by the client. (Anderson & Goolishian, 1992, p. 29)

This "not knowing mind," or "beginner's mind," is echoed in the work of White and Epston (1994), where problems are not situated inside a person and seen as some sort of disease process; rather, the counselor takes a curious stance that aids in revealing the client's theory about what might have led to the construction of their problems. For centuries, Eastern philosophies have discussed the benefit of practicing this beginner's mind. Rather than trying to force change, it is critical to first sit alongside one's experience in observance. In our profession, this stance of awareness allows us to view and ultimately help the client to access their inherent wisdom. This deep knowledge will assist others with recognizing both their capacity and strengths in the face of seemingly insurmountable distress. We encounter people every day where we walk away scratching our heads in wonder as to how they have managed to reach out for support, how they have survived the traumas life brought their way. When we set aside our "expertise" and listen, we are much more likely to help them to find their own answers. In our experience holding this stance, we are consistently amazed by what we discover underneath it all, what has been happening to support survival in effort to find a life worth living in the face of untold adversity. By making the problem the problem instead of the person, we begin to understand the choices they have made in relationship to whatever has disempowered them, thus illuminating what supportive options they have going forward (White & Epston, 1994). A not knowing mind, and an accepting and nonjudgmental mindset, is an essential quality for an empathy that opens space for something other than just the problem and the suffering. As witnesses to this journey, counselors have a unique opportunity to assist others in their own self-healing.

Holding Space

This ability to "hold space" for another is an attunement to the dissonance when two or more conflicting experiences coexist. It requires counselors to hold space for another's experience while also holding on to their own. For example, shame is often a consequence of trauma. It is reflective of the abuse internalized by the person who was abused. It can remind survivors of their flaws, their powerlessness, and, above all, an internal voice of how undeserving they are of anything better. Caring counselors will recognize the impact of trauma and how it partners with shame, what it has robbed them of, and how the symptoms of trauma (e.g., hypervigilance) have separated clients from both loved ones and their own experience of themselves. Respectful counselors will acknowledge the fatigue, understanding how the struggle to feel better is far more about the climb than the climber, but will additionally acknowledge the capacity and right of others to find their own voice in lieu of shame on the other side of suffering. Opening space in this way honors the weight of their histories while also acknowledging inherent capacity for self-healing. From this stance counselors hand over the power for healing where it belongs: to their clients. How quickly counselors can infringe on both the right and necessity of clients to decide for themselves how best to make sense of their pain in the context of their lives.

Empathy

So how does one develop and increase the capacity to have and express empathy effectively? Although the notion of *empathy*, or the capacity to vicariously experience the emotions, cognitions, and sense of self of another, has perhaps been present, even in animals, since the beginning of human interaction, our ability to precisely describe and define this phenomenon has been limited and not always understood across time. According to Lanzoni (2018), the word "empathy" started as a rough translation of the German word *einfuhlung* in 1908. This essentially meant the projection of inner feelings onto inanimate objects, what might be referred to as "animism." Similarly, empathy was described by Freud (1933) as an unconscious identification in reaction to another or object, such as a painting or a score of music. The fears of overidentification prompted early theorists to emphasize the importance of maintaining distance with clients so that their perspectives could be objectively observed, and the experience of their patients would not be unduly influenced. It was this distance that allowed integrity to the therapist's interpretations.

This stance of objectivity was perceived to be unbiased (as if that is possible) and was challenged by Carl Rogers (1957). He contended that empathy was *not* a process of identification, but one that allowed for the suspension, in contrast to abandonment, of one's self. "It is a delicately balanced ability," wrote Katz (1963) in support, "which the empathizer has of being able to plunge into the sea of experience of another person and yet be able to climb out on the shore and regain his [or her] own sense of self" (p. 144). Simply being able to sincerely say "I feel your pain" falls well short of the mark to this type of therapeutic stance.

A balance between understanding the subjective world of the client while still allowing clients the freedom to direct their own lives is central to the Rogerian idea of empathy. This ability to maintain an "as if" therapeutic posture requires the surrendering of one's own experiences and judgment and completely entering into the world of the client (Rogers, 1957). Virginia Satir (1988) elegantly talked about this quality when she wrote, "When I see persons, I see them as human beings who are showing me through their words, affect, and behavior what they have learned about being a person" (p. 516). Empathy, seen this way, empowers clients to see and direct their own lives rather than being something performed by the counselor.

When this quality is lost by counselors, a rapid identification of client experiences can lead to premature problem solving, which, in turn, can lead to harm. This is evident through advice giving, personal examples of success, and soothing statements that attempt to "nurture" others. Although intended to reduce client discomfort, it is likely the discomfort of counselors that is being served. These types of clinical responses not only disempower those we seek to support but also minimize the strengths and resources available to clients and families as they work to confront their challenges in novel ways. If the therapist enters with preconceived notions of interaction, they will be constricted to the needs and world views they personally hold, as opposed to those held by the client (Patterson, 1974).

This point came into full view for me (Bill) in the 1970s. While going to college, I (Bill) found myself working in an inpatient psychiatric hospital. Over the 6 years I spent there, I was employed in many capacities that thrust me into direct patient care. I grew quite fond of this work and the people I had the privilege of serving. During this time there was a man in his 50s from a family that boasted a whole line of people displaying behaviors and speaking of experiences that were apparently quite different from those of the majority. This man (we will call him "Joe") was always polite and stayed pretty much to himself. He never asked to be in the hospital and was admitted on about 10 occasions during my time working there through some sort of court order, involuntarily placing him in our care and requiring him to follow his psychiatrist's treatment prescriptions.

Joe would much rather have been fishing or playing with his grandchildren. Instead, he was having to occupy his time making leather wallets, playing cards and ping pong, eating bland hospital food, and benefiting from an occasional visit by a sympathetic family member. Joe would often have noted in his chart the following phrase, or ones very similar: "The patient was cooperative and polite on contact. His affect appeared flat. He took his medications, attended activities, played ping pong with the staff, and went with the group to the cafeteria for meals." Not much else to say, I guess. After all, Joe did not have much to say himself. Perhaps he had learned that keeping his mouth shut was one possible path available to him for as speedy a discharge as possible. He probably discovered along the way that to discuss his thoughts and perceptions with the staff was to have them recorded in his chart and used as a way of holding him in the hospital longer, thus depriving him of important grandchild visits and time on the water fishing. He played a mean game of ping pong; he had a lot of opportunity to practice due to spending the majority of the prior 20 or so years in various psychiatric hospitals, where the ubiquitous ping pong table continues as a cultural icon. Joe also had learned that the fastest way to gain the favor of the staff was to play ping pong with them, keep the game close, win a few, and let them win more.

Joe had trouble with his doctors. They seemed to insist that he talk about his concerns, and when he complied, he was labeled "delusional," "paranoid," or "thought disordered," as his way of seeing the world was different than those viewed at the time as "normal" or found in that narrowest of range: within normal limits. Although the number of people in the range of "within normal limits" is quite large, the range itself is really quite narrow. Additionally, the definition seemingly changes depending on the view one takes or has. It took Joe years and scores of involuntary commitments to figure out by trial and error what approximated that moving target called "within normal limits." About the time he would seemingly get it right, his doctor would retire, move, or go to another hospital, leaving Joe's care with another psychiatrist with their own definition of what those "normal limits" might be. Unfortunately, each psychiatrist seemed to have their own unique view of this range and shared the notion that it actually defined an immovable, iconic, objective reality like their own private shared psychotic disorder. For Joe it was always a guessing game and one in which he would frequently guess wrong.

Joe was often heard stating his primary goal in life was to be "declared legally sane." He would say something like, "Hell they take me to court and declare me legally insane all the time and put me in these hell holes, so when I act better, why can't they declare me legally sane? It's not fair and it don't make no sense, I tell ya!" There does not appear to be a legal way back to sanity. There are no rituals in place to celebrate a return to that elusive and long-heralded norm of mediocrity. Unfortunately for Joe, and a few million other people, labels describing insanity, once adhered to your forehead, appear to be stuck there permanently. Most societal forces are not really designed to be helpful so much as to inspire compliance and enforce order. This may include commonly understood expressions of empathy in most relationships.

Foucault (1977) described this as "the gaze" and suggested how it keeps everyone in line and moving in the same general direction. He suggested that the metaphor of Bentham's panopticon is fitting, where we are each contained in a cell where it is understood that anyone can be under surveillance at any time—only we are unable to tell when exactly we are being observed and when we are not and thus tend to comport ourselves within the internalized notions of acceptable conduct (Foucault, 1977). Although this notion may serve to explain how cultures are held together and perpetuated, there is also tremendous potential for abuse and oppression, as has been evident throughout history. Who gets to decide what is acceptable? How do we know they are correct? Is there a "correct"?

Who Gets the Last Word?

So often in the art of helping, we ascribe far more emphasis on the worldview and opinions of the "expert" than we do the clients we serve. We minimize their explanatory models and, as mental health professionals, heighten the false accuracy of our own perceptions to the experience of others. Often, our training, emphasizing competence in assessment and theory-driven explanations, breaks people down into diagnostic categories so that problems associated with their pathologies can be addressed. It is a pseudobenevolent "gaze" that seeks to help by helping those who appear incapable of helping themselves. This *illness ideology* portrays people as victims of intrapsychic and biological forces beyond their control and, as such, are in need of benevolent helpers and caregivers in managing their symptoms (Maddux, 2002). From this perspective, clients are in need of experts to guide and instruct them in reducing the progression of their disabling emotional, cognitive, and/or behavioral symptoms. This binary view of change, as in Joe's case, places clients very quickly in a double bind. If they comply with treatment recommendations and arrest the symptoms of their mental illness, then treatment is maintained and the fact of it is reinforced. If they contend that treatment is not needed and/or resist efforts to be treated, they are "resistant" or in "denial" to the severity of their illness, and treatment is still applied. In an effort to be helpful, clients are "gazed at" as helpless and in need of guidance, advice, and prescribed treatments. It is this observational stance that Ross (1977) termed "naïve realism" (p. 754), wherein an observer holds a perspective that assumes objectivity or a lack of bias when observing others. Ross (1977) describes the point of view of naïve realism as:

1. My own perceptions are realistic and "objective" and therefore (reasonable) others will (and should) share them. This illusion of objectivity applies not only to my perceptions of objects and events, but also to beliefs, preferences, priorities, and feelings prompted by those perceptions.

2. I will be able to persuade those who disagree with me, if they are reasonable and open-minded, once I explain what the real facts are and what they really mean.

3. Those who disagree with me, and especially those who challenge the most important beliefs of my group, are unreasonable and/or irrational. They have succumbed to particular sources of bias and error in reasoning. (p. 755)

This description is oddly reminiscent of the position described by psychotherapists over the last 100 years where the "objectivity" of the therapist increased their status in the relationship to being the arbiter of things that are "normal" and those that fall outside of "normal" experiences. Interestingly, early conceptions of empathy resulted in E. Ernest Southard, a Boston neurologist, developing in 1918 what he called the "empathy index" as a tool to diagnose people with schizophrenia wherein the psychiatrist, being objective and unbiased, was able to ascertain if the patient was behaving in a way that could be understood as relatively normal as opposed to those the psychiatrist could not relate to as they were so outside the realm of normal that there was no connection and were therefore considered to be schizophrenic (Lanzoni, 2018). We would suggest that this is an example of what Ross (1977) described as the "fundamental attribution error" before we had a description for it. This is a view that has led us down the road to what might be conceptualized as an egocentric view of people and behavior while ignoring those experiences and knowledge that arise from the lived experience of our clients.

When people from minoritized and/or oppressed groups experience barriers that systematically undermine their ability to access the knowledge, power, resources, and services that would allow them to gain control in their lives, they cannot be expected to function as effectively as those who are enabled by privilege and greater access to social capital (Crether et al., 2008). Informed by the status and science of a profession, and privilege inherent to the roles of psychiatrist, psychologist, or psychotherapist, the right for clients to fully participate in decisions that affect their lives can be, and all too often is, diminished. Rather than an empathic mindset seeking to understand how clients wish to find strength in face of difficulty and stories of past trauma as well as the inherent valor, loyalty, persistence, honesty, prudence, courage, and grief associated with these, mental health professionals can inadvertently embrace a paradigm (or gaze) that oppresses the very freedom clients wish to have more access to. This book promotes the liberatory approaches in our shared professions that elevate the client's voice and lived experience. A resilient and empathic stance is necessary to support people finding their own unique power in relation to whatever trauma (e.g., relational, biological, historical, sociological, generational, etc.) or other oppressive condition they are experiencing or have experienced. People, not therapists, are the experts of their own lives and should always get the last word ... always.

Brief Activity: Sitting in Awareness

We have all sat in the space of self-deprecation and judgment. Self-doubt tracks each of us throughout the day and asks us to question our value in a variety of contexts and interactions. This is also true of the counselor, who may find themselves sitting across from their client, juggling a space of listening to two voices: the client's and their own. As we try to listen to our clients, even with nonjudgment, we all too often find ourselves in an internal conversation, questioning our words, reflections, and ideas. You have likely been in this space, possibly even as you read this book. What could I have done better with my own client who reminds me so much of that example of Joe? The first step is in simply sitting with our own voice, aware that it is there: listening to it, yet not acting. "I wonder if I should have done _____" can shift to "I notice my doubt as I read." There is nothing to do; just listen. As you read this book, listen to what comes up for you. Which of your own lived experiences arise as possible mirrors in bettering your own understanding of yourself? How is my gaze influencing the moment? Then allow yourself the gift of nonjudgment and empathy. There I am. That is me, and that is ok.

Consciousness and Empiricism

The emphasis should be more on helping individual clients use their own resources to change rather than on applying standardized treatment packages.

—*Bohart & Tallman (2010, pp. 99–100)*

K uhn (1970) believed that a paradigm is an intellectual structure seeking to describe the worldview of a professional discipline and that over time, as anomalies accumulate, paradigms are thrown into crisis and change. This chapter will review the intellectual structures that have maintained the paradigm of the counselor as healer—consciousness and empiricism—whereas the following chapter will highlight those "anomalies" that usher in the paradigm of self-healing. The chapter's gaze is focused on the inherent capacity of people and how the counseling relationship can provide space for clients to heal and transform.

Consciousness

In the middle 1800s, human behavior problems were largely conceived as the result of anatomical characteristics (phrenology), brain lesions, faulty morals, mysticism, mesmerism, and hysteria (having a wandering uterus). Psychotherapy techniques consisted mainly of hypnosis, moral teaching and training, and the manipulation of anatomy (Ellenberger, 1970). The focus on the human mind dominated the field and the idea of a self or consciousness began to arise. Ellenberger (1970) suggested that models of the human mind appeared to generally fall into two groups. This idea was called *dispychism*, which was the notion of the mind falling into two distinct parts: an upper conscious and lower conscious. This is similar to the work of Charcot and the phrenologist Gall, known as *polypsychism*, which is the notion that various anatomical aspects have separate egos or personalities that can be disrupted, split, or dissociated through injury outside of what they referred to as the "ego in chief." In the case of Gall, these separate egos resided in anatomical structures of the skull and could be physically manipulated to improve mental health (Murphy & Kovach, 1949/1972). Charcot drew distinctions between hysterical paralysis caused by traumatic events and those caused by some neurological anomaly or lesions (Ellenberger, 1970). Although it is often suggested that Freud "discovered" the unconscious mind, Charcot envisioned trauma as "pathogenic secrets" hidden within the deeper corners of our subconscious decades before Freud and Breuer (1895/1937) published *Studies in Hysteria*. They asserted that their client's "symptoms immediately disappeared without returning if [they] succeeded in thoroughly awakening the memories of the causal process with its accompanying affect, and if the patient circumstantially discussed the process in the most detailed manner and gave verbal expression to the affect" (Breuer & Freud, 1895/1937, pp. 3–4). It was the advent of the "talking cure" where the role of the counselor was to recover unconscious memories and associated emotional experiences. They asserted that although normal memories progress as a story, traumatic or dissociated memories are fragmented. The role of the therapist was to assist clients with putting the pieces together so the story of memory can be told.

This intrapsychic and past focus of psychotherapy remain with us today. This is a structure of thought that suggests painful memories are repressed and, although unavailable to the conscious mind, obtrude in the form of symptoms. In seeking to explain the unexplainable, the consciousness paradigm situates the problem inside the person where the "cure" is in the hands of a skilled arbiter of their reality. Therapists, informed by this paradigm, identify what is wrong with a person so that they may treat the person. It is a perspective that permeates clinical training and practice where, like puzzles, there is something inherently missing within people seeking mental health services and only the expertise of the therapists can determine what is wrong and what can help. Within counseling centers, mental health professionals interact with clients and colleagues using the deficit-based language of this paradigm, focusing on what is going wrong in a client's life. Clients leave such experiences drained, possibly experiencing a lower sense of self-efficacy because of the session's almost exclusive focus on the negative and painful exploration of the past (Saleebey, 2001).

Empiricism

A second paradigm influencing the professional worldview of clinicians is empiricism, emphasizing that all hypotheses and theories must be tested against observation rather than on reasoning, intuition, or revelation alone. It is a foundational shift from the paradigm of consciousness and purports that all we know is known through our senses. It is informed by past experience, and by their simplest parts. In reference to counseling theories, the "reality" of the problems that individuals face results from deficits with how they think and act in reference to both themselves and their environments. Similar to the consciousness paradigm, counselors become objective observers of the mental structures (cognitions) and environmental contingencies (behaviors) representing clients' personal deficits in need of replacement or modification.

Behavioral Perspective

While Freud and Breuer were collaborating in the late 1800s, Ivan P. Pavlov, a Russian physiologist of some note, was researching canine pancreatic nerves and designed his now famous experiments of conditioned reflex by teaching dogs to salivate to the sound of a bell paired with the sight of food (Pavlov, 1928). This discovery gave rise to the growing field of behaviorism. Although Pavlov's work included some notion of unconditioned responses as the primary source of behaviors, it allowed for and emphasized the impact of the environment on behavior. He even suggested that in some of his experiments he witnessed the Lamarckian idea that conditioned responses could somehow be encoded into the heredity of the subject animal (Pavlov, 1928). Pavlov's classical conditioning became a mainstay in psychology and posited that behavior was the result of reinforced responses keying off of basic and perhaps instinctual emotional/physiological reactions like hunger, fear, rage, shame, love, and joy. In 1913, John Watson coined the term "behaviorism" and thus started a major force in psychological thinking and over the next several decades asserted ... wait for it ... *that he could train just about anybody to do and be just about anything.*

In the mid-20th century B. F. Skinner arrived on the scene with extensive research on the antecedents associated with behavior and developed the idea of operant conditioning. He demonstrated and described how various stimuli appear to become paired with other stimuli and how the environment can and does reinforce and shape behaviors in very complex ways. He was able to develop a science of behavior that required little or no understanding of the person. He asserted that as mental health helpers, all we needed to understand was how to manage behavior through the use of reinforcement schedules. It highlighted a perspective that people seek pleasure over pain (i.e., pleasure principle) and established the role of demand characteristics in the environment as the antecedents for behavior as opposed to exclusively internal mental processes (Skinner, 1953).

Similar to the consciousness paradigm, the empirical paradigm of behaviorism elevated the therapist to the role of an expert. Since human behavior is explained in terms of conditioning (without consideration to thoughts or feelings), then all that is needed to help others is to alter behavior patterns. Furthermore, therapists trained in this discipline are perceived to be unbiased and objective, thus holding the power to assert and enforce what is normal behavior and what is aberrant. Behaviors are seen as the outcome of classical and operant reinforcement schedules, where therapists are only required to understand, manage, and change behavior (Skinner, 1953). In contrast to the consciousness paradigm, empirical behaviorism called into question the notion of diagnoses and other trait theories by suggesting they represented circular logical fallacies and provided little, if any, information of significance in understanding and influencing behavior. For example, if we suggest a person behaves in a certain way because they suffer from the mental disorder called "depression" or "major depressive disorder" and we ask why they are suffering, the answer is because they show the symptoms for this disorder. If we inquire further, we are told that the person has this problem (signs and symptoms) because they have major depressive disorder, and so it goes around and around without ever really giving us something useful to understand and intervene effectively. The behaviorists viewed the question of why a behavior exists as perhaps interesting but of little use in managing or changing behavior. They posed questions that asked *how* behaviors happen and *what* maintains them (see Appendix A).

The influence of behaviorism still resonates within the mental health field today. By influencing the inherent power of therapists to assess and orchestrate behavioral interventions, the need for developing empathic relationships and emphasizing the worldview and strengths of clients is diminished. Token economies are still widely used in inpatient settings, and the pressure for mental health agencies to demonstrate empirically supported treatments (EST) means that clinicians are more likely to focus on manualized treatment protocols rather than the inherent strengths of clients or the healing nature of quality therapeutic relationships.

Cognitive Perspective

Around the same time as Skinner developed his ideas, a couple of clinicians came along pointing to irrational thoughts and cognitive distortions as the source of emotional and behavioral distress. Albert Ellis (1975) developed what he called rational emotive behavior therapy (REBT) and contended that, in contrast to the consciousness paradigm, no matter how much insight an individual attained, they rarely lost their symptoms. He suggested there were mediating cognitive influences on behaviors, that people constructed such deep-rooted dysfunctional demands on themselves, and that only a directive approach from the therapist could uproot them. Taking a slightly more collaborative approach, Beck, A. T. Beck (1979) argued that counselors help people (a) identify cognitive rules and life hypotheses, (b) test the validity of these hypotheses, and (c) modify the rules and/or life hypotheses. Both Ellis and Beck advanced the empirical paradigm with their notions about executive function and cognitive science, emphasizing four essential truths still informing cognitive behavioral therapy (CBT) today:

- Humans perceive, think, emote, and behave simultaneously where all actions are implicit to the rules of their thinking.
- Unhappiness is directly related to the rules/beliefs associated with life events and stressors.
- Since cognitions create our behavior, people have the ability to recognize, dispute, and change maladaptive beliefs.
- The intent of the cognitive therapist, therefore, is to identify client thought patterns that are maladaptive and replace them with those that reduce stress and increase life satisfaction.

From a CBT perspective, the therapist is again positioned as the expert who can show the way for those having difficulties by examining how they acquired their irrational beliefs and cognitive distortions, implementing challenges to them, and substituting rationality to decisions about how they are going to behave. If they can stop the thought, they can stop the behavior, and if they stop the behavior, they can eliminate the problem—a benevolent and noble pursuit.

Empirically Supported Treatments

Grounded in the empirical paradigm are research protocols seeking to determine efficacy in the treatment of mental health disorders. Successful outcomes are determined when comparing the randomized treatment participants with a no-treatment control group, alternate treatment group, or placebo and there is a significant statistical difference. As an empirical model, treatments that lend themselves to EST methodology are behavioral and cognitive therapeutic approaches. Viewing the role of a counselor as essentially a teacher and expert guide, these therapies have adopted manuals to ensure the consistency of treatment to all participants. Mental health institutions, seeking to provide evidence-based practices as well as secure funding incentives by doing so, utilize ESTs that primarily include variations of the behavioral and cognitive paradigms. Dialectical behavioral therapy (DBT), a related and more recent popular model, works from a sophisticated and creative combination of prior models with an emphasis on CBT and ultimately exposure therapy. In this model patients are prepared for therapy by teaching them basic skills that are categorized as "mindfulness," "distress tolerance," "emotional regulation," and "interpersonal effectiveness" (Linehan,

1993). The underlying assumption of this model is that somehow a person was unable or denied the opportunity to obtain the necessary skills to navigate life in the long term effectively and instead learned an alternate short term and potentially less effective set of skills to survive. The model supports the notion that we all do the best we can under adverse and traumatic circumstances to survive and get our needs met. Also, the more outside of "normal" the experience of development, the more maladaptive behaviors emerge to cope. Once again, we encounter the gaze of society. Who determines what is outside of normal experience?

For several years, the American Psychiatric Association's (APA, 1987) *Diagnostic and Statistical Manual of Mental Disorders* (DSM) included in the diagnosis of posttraumatic stress disorder a requirement that a person experience an event that was "outside of normal experience." This definition tended to restrict consideration of everyday experiences of the vast majority of people today and throughout history. Trauma has been and is a part of life. Although not a welcome part, it is nonetheless something that occurs at one time or another for everyone. Under the DBT model, we must get a person ready for therapy by providing them with the skills they need in order to be successful in therapy before doing therapy. Although the model is well defined and considered an empirically supported treatment model (this may be due to the narrow definition used for positive outcomes), it elevates the therapist, once again, as the arbiter of reality. It may resemble a crisis management approach to therapy as opposed to one where autonomy and self-efficacy are assumed. The client is again seen as damaged goods and in need of repair or rehabilitation. Coincidently, DBT was originally developed to combat suicidal behavior and what Linehan (1993) described as *parasuicidal behavior,* or behavior that results in changing an emotional state by engaging in self-harm behaviors that can, over time, exhaust local medical resources.

Client as Healer

Sexton (2007) stated that the idea that simply because a treatment is manualized means that it will be mechanical and unresponsive to client needs is unjustified. However, relationship factors, client qualities, and the importance of cultural and social support systems have been largely ignored in the EST research. Furthermore, it continues to accentuate the importance of counselor judgment and diminishes what actually works in naturalistic settings. In his exhaustive review of outcomes studies in counseling, Norcross (2009/2019) concluded that the only significant predictor of positive clinical outcome under the purview of therapists was the quality of the counseling relationship as experienced by clients. Evidence suggested that the client's perception of the therapeutic bond and agreement to the goals and tasks of therapy predicted eventual positive outcome (Duncan et al., 2010). Hope, (Frank & Frank, 1991), self-determination (Scheel, 2011), and unique client strengths (Cuijpers et al., 2012) have also demonstrated clinical improvement.

CBT brought with it from the behavioral scientists a reductionistic ease where ideas could be operationalized for use in quantitative research, sparking the rise of the evidence-based treatment (EBT) models of today. As a binary view of the human experience, wellness becomes the absence of disease; behavior is assessed as appropriate/functional or inappropriate/dysfunctional; and cognitions are represented by those that are rational in contrast to those that are irrational and/or self-defeating. With an inherent simplicity, this gaze of the human experience contends that (a) normal and abnormal are a measurable reality, (b) people receiving counseling must have a clinical disorder, and (c) the counselor is an unbiased perceiver of these realities and an accurate judge of disorders (Fong, 1993). From this perspective, clients are broken, fragmented, and in need of experts to prescribe and instruct them in reducing the progression of their disabling emotional, cognitive, and/or behavioral symptoms. However, a more hopeful view of humankind arose during this period, a paradigm that saw people as capable, reflective, and flourishing when access to caring and respectful relationships are available. In this paradigm, clients, not counselors, are the healers in their own lives.

Top Takeaways from Chapters 1 and 2

The first chapter highlighted the impact that early intellectual structures have had on maintaining a paradigm that healing in therapy is primarily influenced by the expertise of the counselor. We traced the evolution of psychodynamic approaches, behaviorism, cognitive behavioral therapy, and the notion of empathy and examined how relational dynamics in psychotherapy are central to the healing process as well as a necessary condition for effective counseling. In the 20th century the evolution to the ideas of consciousness and empiricism have inadvertently overemphasized the role and worldview of the clinician at the expense of the personal qualities and resources of the client as well as the ability of the counseling relationship to provide a holding environment for reflection, understanding, and risk taking associated with transformational change and renewal—the essence of resilience-centered counseling. The top takeaways from Chapters 1 and 2 are:

- The only significant predictor to positive counseling outcomes that are clearly under the influence of the therapist, regardless of theoretical orientation, are relational dynamics (Norcross & Lambert, 2019; Norcross, 2011; Hubble et al., 2004; Duncan et al., 2010).

- The *illness ideology* of mental illness portrays people as victims of intrapsychic and biological forces beyond their control and, as such, in need of benevolent helpers and caregivers in managing their symptoms (Maddux, 2002). From this perspective, patients are in need of experts to guide and instruct them in reducing the progression of their disabling emotional, cognitive, and/or behavioral symptoms.

- The influence of behaviorism and the profound role of environmental demand characteristics continues to resonate within the mental health field today. By influencing the inherent power of therapists to assess and orchestrate behavioral interventions, the need for developing empathic relationships and emphasizing the worldview and strengths of clients is often diminished.

- Relationship factors, client qualities, and the importance of cultural and social support systems have been largely ignored in the evidence-based treatment and empirically supported treatment research.

- The counseling relationship has the potential to empower and motivate people in the process of change. Insight and change, therefore, become less about the expertise of therapists and the theoretical formulations informing their actions and more about the inherent resilient qualities individuals and families tap into in their struggles toward a better life.

Appendix A. Behavioral Functional Analysis: Teacher Interview Sequence
Adapted from Kampwirth (1999)

Activity

Consider a child/teen displaying "excessive disruptiveness." Break into pairs, have one partner play the role of a teacher who has referred a student for what he calls *disruptive behaviors,* and the other partner play the role of the school counselor/consultant who attempts to engage the teacher to be more specific about the behavior of concern utilizing the interview questions below. Note: the school counselor/consultant will need to take notes during the interview for later analysis.

Behavioral Interview Sequence

1. Tell me more about your concerns about the student.

2. Please give me an example of this behavior. What is it like, typically? Who else is involved in it?

3. What seems to bring it on? What causes it? What circumstances are occurring when it happens?

4. What do you do, typically, when it occurs? What has been the result of these responses?

5. You have described settings in which it occurs. Are there times when it does not occur? What is different about those times?

6. What is your goal for this student and these behaviors? Which behaviors do you wish to reinforce (i.e., see more of), and which do you wish to ignore or discourage (i.e., extinguish)?

7. Given what you know about this behavior and what you have tried up to now, what do you believe would be a good approach to take at this time? What do you believe is the best thing to do at this time?

Self-Healing

We who lived in concentration camps can remember the men who walked through the huts comforting others, giving away their last piece of bread. They may have been few in number, but they offer sufficient proof that everything can be taken from [someone] but one thing: the last of the human freedoms—to choose one's attitude in any given set of circumstances, to choose one's way.

—Frankl (1949, p. 65)

For people seeking counseling for the first time, the experience is often met with worried anticipation. The thought of being asked to recount the worst parts of their loved ones or themselves during life's most desperate moments can be overwhelming. Sharing these experiences with a counselor, experiences often mired in shame and fear, is to risk the same level of judgment already burdened on themselves. From a consciousness or empiricist paradigm, counselors may see client emotional expressions as patterns of pathology rather than patterns of resilience. If others are perceived as broken by their histories, helpers will find only what is wrong with clients. They will see only that which needs "fixing" and seek to reduce suffering by diagnosing the problem and prescribing treatment. Albeit benevolent, counselors will equate the severity of life's painful events to the people having experienced them. Heider (1958), in explaining the tenets of attribution theory, concluded that in the end, people act according to their beliefs. If counselors believe themselves to be healers, they will likely see only wounds. In their efforts to "help clients feel better," they will have missed opportunities to see client strengths and partner with them to "become stronger."

In this chapter we will pick up on the history and evolution of various psychotherapy and counseling approaches and extend our discussion into the types of meaningful change that make real differences in the lives of the people who seek psychotherapy. Our view will turn toward counseling paradigms contending that clients are self-governing. We will review intellectual structures that seek to understand people's capacity for self-healing and the inherent benefit of dissonance, uncertainty, and the importance of considering change in second- and third-order perspectives. By looking to the resources people bring to the therapeutic encounter, change not only becomes possible but also becomes inevitable. Like the transforming power of water on an arid landscape, attuning to resilient patterns allows the unspoken part of all of us to blossom.

Finally, this chapter will explore the importance of counselors helping others take stock of themselves while anchoring a forward flag toward a preferred vision of their better selves. This is the foundation of resilience-centered counseling. Like all courageous expeditions, prior to the first step, attention to the ground beneath one's feet is required. Beginning with the end in mind, in service to these personal and social values, is where self-healing is found and the ability to withstand life's tribulations is discovered.

Self-Healing

Although self-healing is heralded as a central dynamic in most therapeutic approaches, it is overshadowed by an emphasis on counselor-initiated interventions. Counseling theories have long been considered accurate reflections of the human experience, where the problems individuals face result from their deficits in thought, ability, or in reaction to life events. Deficit-based models contend that clients are either helpless in the face of difficulties and/or have somehow acted/responded improperly when difficult situations arose. Most models to date spend inordinate amounts of energy describing the problems as embodied in, and as the fault of, the client. Yet we never seem to give the client credit for surviving the difficulties and moving past the issues confounding them during therapy (or outside of therapy). Whether by increasing rationality, shaping behaviors, or interpreting the influence of psychic forces, counselors often see themselves as "holding the key" to client and/or family change. Differentiating the self-healing potential of clients from therapist procedures has inadvertently increased client dependence on therapy.

As noted in the previous chapter, much of counseling theory has placed great emphasis on the skills, expertise, and armamentarium of the clinician. The structure of the session, the assessment of presenting concerns, and prescription of a treatment plan accentuate the importance of the counselor as the healer in therapy rather than the client. The impression that clients are capable of fixing themselves has been largely overshadowed by empirical models emphasizing client change as a product of therapist interventions, expertise, and following manual treatment guidelines. The enthusiasm for applying specific techniques persists even though the evidence suggests they demonstrate little influence on overall counseling outcomes (Duncun et al., 2010). The emergence of ESTs and the emphasis on specific techniques in therapy suggest the "paradoxical power of paradigms over data in scientific research psychology, even though the positivist paradigm is purportedly data driven!" (Fishman, 1999, p. 233). It is as the Chinese proverb explained: Give a man a fish, and he eats for a day; teach him to fish, and he eats for lifetime.

In contrast, the belief that people are themselves the hero of their own story is the cornerstone to the existential and humanist movement. This is a shift away from the "magic" of therapist driven interventions and toward the assertion that clients within empathic counseling relationships will seek self-healing as the ultimate therapeutic outcome. Approaches from this paradigm envision the counseling relationship as a nonjudgmental container in support of the natural inclinations toward growth harboring an unfaltering optimism in the human spirit to heal even the most traumatic wounds. The following is a review of the principles of self-healing as noted in the tenets of counseling theory and neurobiology: self-actualizing tendencies, the experience of meaning, and the inherent restorative capacities in all of us.

Self-Actualizing Tendencies

The humanistic and existential movements in psychotherapy and counseling took root in the middle of the 20th century, emphasizing empathy and the development of a trusting therapeutic relationship. Otto Rank (1932) viewed the client, not the counselor, as the central figure in the healing process. From his perspective, people were not victims of the past defined by faulty actions or beliefs but capable of self-healing even in the face of overwhelming adversity. The aim of therapy was not a battle ground between the id and superego or the rejection of cognitive distortions or actions, but access to existing creative personal powers to aid in their understanding, acceptance, and intrinsic capacity for self-growth. He respected the ability of others to course correct and believed that experiencing themselves in the present, or the "here/now," provided an understanding of not just the lived stories but the experience of themselves. He cautioned counselors to be neither an instrument of love (where dependence might ensue) nor an instrument of education (where manipulation might exist). Considering the trends at the time, Rank (1941) was concerned that psychology was far too focused on controlling and directing people. He characterized psychotherapy as promising to "cure everything in the other which we dislike" (Rank, 1941, p. 44). He asserted, in repudiation with most of his contemporaries at the time, that clients, not counselors, were most important to therapeutic change.

Carl Rogers, in his first book, *Counseling and Psychotherapy* (1942), and later in his book *Client-Centered Therapy* (1951), also believed that people were self-directing. He coined the term "person-centered therapy" in the 1960s and reduced the role of the therapist as expert to facilitator in the psychotherapy process. He elevated the client's experience, disliked diagnosis, and asserted a positive orientation toward the nature of human beings. He argued that problems are found in our perceptions as opposed to some sort of illness (Rogers, 1977). Rogers (1961) also claimed that all human activity is an attempt to become a better person and that we are predisposed to move in what we perceive to be positive directions. He further believed we all have a primary need to realize our full potential, contending that if nonnurturing environments cause problems for people, then nurturing environments and relationships will likely serve to facilitate change (Rogers, 1967).

The importance of these nurturing environments was the cornerstone of Maslow's (1943) hierarchy of needs. Represented by a pyramid (see Figure 3.1), individuals must meet their needs at a foundational level first (physiological, safety and security, love and belonging, and self-worth) before being motivated sufficiently to address their growth needs (self-understanding, aesthetic, and self-actualization). As Maslow

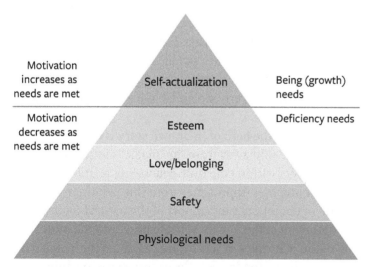

FIGURE 3.1 Maslow's Hierarchy of Needs
(Source: https://www.simplypsychology.org/maslow.html)

(1962) imagined it, growth needs are the enduring motivation for seeking more from oneself. As an instinctual drive, and if provided the right conditions, people strive to make the most of themselves—in essence, to attain their fullest potential, as Maslow, Rogers, and Rank imagined.

Carl Rogers made empathy, or the experience of it, the central tenant of counseling and one of the curative qualities of therapy. The aim of Rogerian therapy was to assist others in developing a greater degree of internal locus of control so that they might take charge of their life (Rogers, 1961). To have an internal locus of control is to participate in one's own fate rather than feeling victimized by it. He maintained that if a counselor could create the following conditions during therapy, clients would self-actualize and begin to govern their lives:

- Two persons are in psychological contact.
- The first, whom we shall term the client, is in a state of incongruence, being vulnerable or anxious.
- The second person, whom we shall term the therapist, is congruent or integrated in the relationship.
- The therapist experiences unconditional positive regard for the client.
- The therapist experiences an empathic understanding of the client's internal frame of reference and endeavors to communicate this experience to the client.
- The communication to the client of the therapist's empathic understanding and unconditional positive regard is to a minimal degree achieved. (Rogers,1957)

Rogers viewed these conditions as both sufficient and necessary in psychotherapy. His work gave rise to interests in training and assessing empathic capacities in psychotherapists. Two researchers attempted to answer this need. Carkhuff and Truax (1967) developed empathy scales to be used in counselor training programs that initially identified nine levels of empathic responding, which was reduced to eight and then five levels: Low Level of Empathic Responding (Level 1); Moderately Low Level of Empathic Responding (Level 2); Interchangeable or Reciprocal Level of Empathic Responding (Level 3); Moderately High Level of Empathic Responding (Level 4); and High Level of Empathic Responding (Level 5). The counselors-in-training would have their session recorded and rated by trained practitioners with this scale to assess their level of skill and progress in acquiring increased abilities at empathic responding.

Ironically, Rogers (1957) contended that an empathic presence was not a technique. He argued that "playing the role of the therapist" and "being a therapist" were qualitatively different. "Intellectual training," wrote Rogers (1957), "and the acquiring of information has, I believe, many valuable results—but becoming a therapist is not one of those results" (p. 101). In other words, the level of empathy established and maintained with a client is ultimately found within the character of the counselor. The counselor needs to have a special sensitivity to clients' hopes, fears, tensions, needs, and beliefs (Patterson, 1974). That sensitivity is relationally motivated, where the counselor is a facilitative companion characterized "by an acceptance of this other person as a separate person with value in [their] own right, and by a deep empathic understanding ... to see [their] private world" (Rogers as cited in Katz, 1963, p. 4). An empathic stance by counselors, rather than a toolbox of interventions, is considered the essential factor for stimulating client healing.

Rogers also became involved with translating his work to group leadership. He defined the role of a leader to include giving autonomy to persons in the group with the freedom to "do their own thing," stimulating independence in thought and action in the members, accepting the "unacceptable" through innovative creations that emerge within the group, encouraging and relying on self-evaluation, and finding reward in the development and achievement of others. He suggested that the ultimate goal of any group leader is to become a participant (Rogers, 1977), where the group experience is both collaborative and mutually influential between group members and group leaders. It is an interactive process that has the capacity to benefit all who are involved.

Today, postmodern therapists, as well as most others of Rogers's time and since, embrace the main tenet that people are endowed with self-actualizing tendencies that can be triggered through empathic connection with others. The idea of "meeting the client where the client is" reached maturity under Rogers's watchful eye, and he remains one of the most influential practitioners in the history of psychotherapy. A recent counselor-trainee noted to me (Colin) recently:

> After learning about the myriad theories, finding the theories that resonate with my internal orientation, and being nearly complete with my academic courses, this training reminds me of my intention as I began this program: to honor and reflect back to clients their inherent goodness, worthiness of love, and their resilience even in the depth of their greatest struggles. This course helped me to settle more deeply into my own presence as a critical counseling tool. I fully expect it will take intentionality and tenacity to notice myself reverting back into thinking and intellectualizing because I spent so much of my life in this place. But I have had the experience of the deeper connections that come from a more heart and somatic based way of being connected to myself. (Jessie)

The Experience of Meaning

Viktor Frankl, a Jewish Austrian psychiatrist, published *Man's Search for Meaning* in 1949 recounting his experiences during the Holocaust when he and his family were imprisoned in the Nazi death camps. Frankl was the sole member of his family to survive. His therapy model resembled significant aspects of exposure therapy decades before it became a mainstay in trauma treatment. His work marks the beginning of the existential therapy movement that sought to empower clients to help themselves by finding meaning in their life regardless of their life circumstances. Frankl (1949) noted that those who have a "why" to live can bear almost any "how." Emphasizing the importance of freewill, Frankl provided existential therapists an early window into an unwavering belief in the resilient nature of people: that we are defined not by what happens to us but by how we grapple with it. Resilience, from this perspective, rises out of the rigors of living—a "leaning into" anxiety, stress, and fear as necessary in finding insight, courage, personal freedom, and, ultimately, meaning.

In agreement, Rollo May (1950) believed that "meeting with anxiety" can free us from boredom and provide personal insight for seeing life with sharpness and clarity. He encouraged clients to embrace the uncomfortable and to overcome the natural urges to avoid, deny, or distract. As noted in his open letter to Carl Rogers regarding "the problem with evil":

> In my experience, our human adventures from cradle to grave take on a zest, a challenge, an attractiveness when we see and affirm this human potentiality of both good

and evil. The joy we experience will have, as its other pole, the self-assertion, the hostility, the negative possibilities that I have been talking about. In my experience it is this polarity, this dialectical interaction, this oscillation between positive and negative that gives the dynamic and depth to human life. Life, to me, is not a requirement to live out a preordained pattern of goodness, but a challenge coming down through the centuries out of the fact that each of us can throw the lever toward good or toward evil. (May, 1982, pp. 19–20)

From this perspective, existential living is a daily exercise of freewill highlighting the inner experience of people's lives rather than merely a telling of the experience. It embodies a belief that benefit can be derived by embracing both pain and joy, a premise inconsistent with most medical and empirical paradigms as well as within our everyday interactions. If one were to say, "I don't feel very good about myself. What's the point?" others around them might seek to talk them out of it or persuade them that their experience of themselves is fallible. It implies a fear that this way of thinking must be avoided, increasing both the strength and persistence of the oppressive way of thinking (Wegner & Bargh, 1998). From the binary gaze of empiricism, health is the absence of disease where treatment seeks to avoid those actions or thoughts that might trigger a "relapse." Farley (2008) contended that apathy, emptiness, and depression occur when one fails to acknowledge the pain, anxiety, and unmet needs reflective of the human experience. It is a "living with paradox" whereby embracing that which is being avoided allows space for something else to emerge. To consider only treatment is to ignore the wisdom that might emerge from the pain avoided.

Activity: Experience of Anxiety and Meaning

In the human experience, no one is free from suffering. Life can challenge us in ways that we least expect, and in these moments, we find ourselves feeling "ill prepared," as if there is something we could have done or controlled to avoid the pain. Yet when we think back on some of our deepest moments of growth and learning, they often emerge out of some of the harshest of conditions. What empowers us to learn, upon hindsight, is rarely something that someone said or told us to think or feel. It is a reflection in the mirror, where, over time, we find ourselves stronger simply by surviving. That vantage that we gain with time is actually a relationship within ourselves and likely the outcome of many conversations: internal with ourselves (conscious and subconscious) and external with others in our support network. When we seek to avoid painful experiences out of the natural instinct to survive, there is nothing wrong with us; we are being human. Yet when courage meets that desire to avoid, we may find ourselves stronger than before. In this way, it is the existence of fear that drives us to courage and to the choice to face challenges, to connect to ourselves, and to reach out to others. When our clients find us, they are already on that path for themselves, and in our work, we should honor those first steps as the critical baseline of resilience.

Take a moment to think back on a time in your life where you faced a depth of hardship that scared you, a time where you felt so anxious that you did not know what to think, feel, or do next. Think back on how you took a breath, had the courage to take next steps, and someone in your network witnessed your courage. They likely did not climb the mountain for you, but in their witnessing of your climb, you gained the strength to keep going. They saw you, and so you too, might see yourself.

Greenberg and Paivio (1997) noted that by gradually assisting clients to access and experience the intense shame surrounding their history of abuse, a healthy anger may surface. As a voice of self-respect, they noted clients neither reverted to the same level of shame nor became overly focused on their anger but found a level of understanding. They needed space for the addition, rather than the absence, of other ways of viewing themselves and others. Gestalt therapists have long asserted that authentic change only occurs by acknowledging and accepting all parts of oneself. In fact, Rogers (1995) noted that only when people accept themselves can change occur. In his study of patients with terminal cancer, Irvin Yalom (1980) found a similar paradox. He explained that death anxiety was proportional to life satisfaction and wrote:

> When life appeared satisfying, dying was less troublesome. ... Lesser satisfaction with past life went with a more troubled view of the illness and its outcome. The lesser the life satisfaction, the greater was the depression, anxiety, anger, and overall concern about the Illness. ... The results seem counterintuitive because, on the superficial level, one might conclude that the unsatisfied and disillusioned might welcome the respite of death. But the opposite is true: a sense of fulfillment, a feeling that life has been well lived, mitigates against the terror of death. (Yalom, 1980, p. 208)

From an existential gaze, to relieve suffering is to first lessen the fear of it. For those recovering from traumatic events, attempts at emotional numbing are natural reactions when the person's coping resources are overwhelmed (Joseph, 2010). Although this coping strategy is helpful in the short term, it is like grasping sand: The harder you squeeze to keep it contained, the more likely it is to seep out in ways that can harm ourselves and others. Unresolved fears can interfere with relationships, impact the fundamental beliefs about oneself and others, cause people to question their place in the world, and dramatically disrupt the nervous system. These patterns of avoidance are the mind's way of protecting itself when the body's stress response system is overwhelmed (van der Kolk, 2015).

Restorative Capacities

During a perceived threat, our sympathetic nervous system mobilizes our body to respond through the release of hormones (e.g., adrenaline, cortisol, epinephrine, and norepinephrine). This survival reaction takes the shape of either fighting back, taking flight, or freezing when rendered helpless by an overwhelming force (Herman, 1997). All neurochemical energy is shifted away from the more evolved parts of the brain required for higher order functioning (e.g., prefrontal and orbitofrontal cortex) and diverted to the more reptilian parts of the brain needed for survival (e.g., brain stem, basal ganglia, and thalamus). Individuals become hypervigilant to the world around them, unable to access parts of the brain needed for self-regulation. They will also lose the ability to communicate normally. Their words will become limited, accelerated, and harsher, and events will be remembered in fragments since the part of the brain needed for assigning meaning and linking experiences together is inaccessible (Dubi et al., 2017).

Once the threat ceases, the parasympathetic nervous system (PNS) kicks the body into restorative mode through the release of gamma-aminobutyric acids. These acids bind with the synaptic membranes, making them less likely to conduct the electrical charge needed to respond to the stress cues

(Gunnar & Vazquez, 2006). These "vertical structures of the brain" reduce stress hormones and allow the brain to shift from a bottom-up processing back to the normal top-down structure of experiencing the world (see Figure 3.2 below). When a threat is not perceived, the parasympathetic nervous system is active and we have more access to calm, comfort, and satisfaction as well as an increased tolerance for dissonance and uncertainty.

Similar to the definition of resilience, the ability to bounce back from adversity (Tugade & Frederickson, 2004) is a restorative capacity in all of us. Adversity stimulates a natural protective response and, when the threat is over, a return to homeostasis, or balance. Central to recovery, and

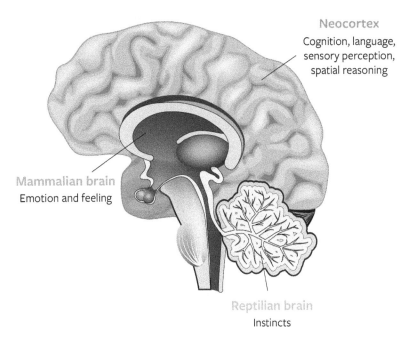

FIGURE 3.2 Vertical Structures of the Brain
(Copyright © 2019 Depositphotos/edesignua)

an essential dynamic of self-healing, is the activation of the PNS. By learning to attune to flow with anxiety and release muscular tension is to invite in a growing tolerance for interpersonal dissonance. This is consistent with the outcome research of Gentry et al. (2015) in their review of evidence-based competencies for trauma counselors. They concluded that developing empathic and warm clinical relationships helped clients experience a felt sense of safety in order to reduce their muscular tension and heart rate. Learning to access this relaxed state and bounce back from SNS triggers is an essential component prior to engaging in recommended exposure-based approaches (EMDR, narrative, etc.). In other words, supporting the self-healing and actualizing tendencies of clients is to provide empathic counseling relationships that trust in their inherent strengths and the capacity in learning to tolerate extreme dissonance rather than avoid it. As Sharon Stanley (2006) wrote, "When people suffering from trauma are able to stay embodied and regulate their affective states, they can tolerate small doses of suffering and pain while processing traumatic memories" (p. 8).

Bamboo Tree

The experience of self-healing is much like the bamboo tree: Although the root system is slow to become established, once it does, it becomes one of the fastest growing plants in the world. Learning to regulate and tolerate the protective emotions of adversity and trauma can be a series of incremental steps. However, once this somatic balance is experienced, executive functions of the brain have access to assist others with making sense of the unimaginable and unexplainable. Self-healing and resilient living become nourished and can grow exponentially.

Autonomic nervous system

Sympathetic *When we are stressed*	**Parasympathetic** *When we are relaxed*
Activates the body's defense mechanisms preparing for flight, fight, or freezing.	Activates the "relaxing" or balancing system.
As a stress response: • Increased heart rate • Decreased stomach activity • Pupils dilate • Glucose is released	As a balancing response: • Decreased heart rate • Increased stomach activity • Pupils contract • Glucose is stored

FIGURE 3.3 Autonomic Nervous System

An Example

Recently, a 28-year-old transgender female-identifying client who reported struggling with Bipolar 1 disorder since adolescence and who had been stable on medication for several years complained to me (Bill) that, "I think my medication interferes with my femininity when I am getting manic!" Let's call her Joanne. I braced myself for an explanation of why she is going to stop taking her medication because it interferes with who she is. This is a not uncommon concern with people who struggle with this issue of mania and dramatic mood swings. I have heard it for years usually preceding a decompensation or crash of some kind. My prior experiences have convinced me that this is one of the biggest dangers facing people who manage life with medication assistance. I prepared to confront this danger and decided instead to ask a question.

Bill: Could tell me more about that?

Joanne: Well, it's like you know how Lithium sort of gives you a second to think about what you want to do before you do it? Especially when I feel the mania it like slows me down enough that I get to think about what I want to do instead of just doing it.

Bill: Okay and ...

Joanne: Well, the other day I was dressed to the nines and felt really good about how I looked before going out, knock out dress, really feminine, you know, and I was walking by the mirror and looked at myself and thought 'I can't go out like this!' and I went and changed my clothes to be more conservative. It was depressing you know, and that is how I think it interferes!

Bill: That is a difficult situation, and it creates a real dilemma for you ...

Joanne: Yeah, it sucked, I couldn't be who I wanted to be! It got me thinking that maybe I could take one less pill a day you know, sort of a compromise where I could get some of the control I need and still be able to let go a little and be myself, right?! And then I realized I tried that a few times before and it turned out to be a disaster. Things always went sideways real fast and got away from me.

Bill: So where does that leave you?

Joanne: I have to decide—do I want to be more of myself, or do I want to be that person who feels like punching my Dad in the face and does it--or do I want to be that person who might feel like punching my Dad in the face and decides not to and just feels like it and dresses a bit more conservatively and a little less of myself.

Bill: Wow! Or I wonder if you could dress more like yourself, more feminine and be uncomfortable with it and go out anyway because you decided to do that.

Joanne: Weird right! I guess I could not let the mirror make my decisions and still stay out of disasters that happen when I don't take the Lithium. I think it [the medicine] lets me decide for myself.

Bill: Are you suggesting that Lithium helps you live consciously, gives you that second between doing what you want and what you think you should do? Like you grew up with heteronormative values that conflict with who you feel you are today, and the medication slows things down enough for you to feel some discomfort with who you are and at the same time allows you to also decide what you want to do in the face of self-destructive impulses? Now you get to decide and before it felt like there were no choices.

Joanne: Something like that yes, I think so … like I get to decide what I am going to do instead of people who piss me off or mirrors deciding for me!

I could have gone with my gut feeling, professional expertise, and experience and tried to head Joanne off in what I was thinking was a justification to stop taking medication to manage mania and dramatic mood swings. I could have challenged Joanne to see it my way. There are times I would have done just that and felt fine about it. I could have let my expertise interfere with Joanne's accomplishments and indigenous wisdom. I didn't, I let Joanne explain, I joined with her in her effort to sort it out and understand it in her own terms which she did far better than I could ever have accomplished on her behalf.

When counselors view their clients as having the capacity for self-healing, they hold meaningful space in an open attitude toward emotions, thoughts, and sensations where negative emotions and life challenges are viewed as an inevitable part of the human experience. These are often reflective of developmental changes in identity and social roles, daily life stressors, and a striving to organize a life built around meaningful goals and values. The essence of working meaningfully with others is to become less concerned about the story itself and more concerned about how the story influences the storyteller: an attunement to what is being experienced of what is being said.

Top Takeaways

1. The centerpiece in client-centered therapy is empathy and joining with the other, the idea of meeting the client where the client has reached maturity under the therapist's watchful eye. Today postmodern therapists, as well as most others of Rogers's time and since, embrace most of what he asserted as the primary conditions for growth and effective therapy. He remains one of the most influential practitioners in the history of psychotherapy.

2. When we walk alongside anxiety and fear, we give companionship to stress and heartache, which, in turn, allows the space for courage and healing to open.

3. Clients have the capacity to heal and grow in the face of their own life struggles.

4. The counselor is not the expert, but the companion, on the journey to client healing.

5. Resilience is defined by a naturally occurring restorative system in the face of trauma and stress, as noted in the interplay between the sympathetic nervous system response to stress and the parasympathetic nervous system in restoring balance once the threat has lessened. One way to activate this response in an inward attunement within the empathic presence of another.

Interdependency

The teaching and learning of structure, rather than simply the mastery of facts and techniques, is at the center of the classic problem of transfer. ... If earlier learning is to render later learning easier, it must do so by providing a general picture in terms of which the relations between things encountered earlier and later are made as clear as possible.

—Jerome Bruner (1990, p. 12)

Thus far, we have been discussing the nature of healing and the necessity of counselors to provide empathic spaces whereby clients "hold the discomfort" in order to come to terms with life adversities. From this therapeutic stance, meaningful change occurs when all sides of an experience can be examined. Where there are deficits, there are also strengths; where problems arise, there are preferences; where there is resistance, there is also inspiration; and where despair resides, hope and resilience also live. From this perspective, understanding occurs not by carving an experience into smaller parts but by understanding how the parts intersect to form the experience as a whole. This idea where the "whole is greater than the sum of its parts" was first introduced by early field theorists. A gaze central to a resilient centered stance with others.

In 1923, Max Wertheimer rejected the idea that behavior and perception could be broken down into parts and then reassembled to solve life problems, as purported by behavioral empiricists. Through his study on apparent movement (phi phenomenon) where vertical and horizontal strips were seen not in isolation but in relationship to one another, he claimed that perception occurs in concert with the environment. Together with Wolfgang Kohler (1925) and Kurt Koffka (1935), they founded the school of Gestalt psychology. These theorists saw the Gestalt as an active process whereby people seek to fill gaps between the parts of an experience so that the whole of it can be fully perceived and acted upon. Past and present experiences affect perception where "individuals do not perceive the components of the experience but give a meaning to the whole input" (Bolles, 1991, p. 21). These are governed by a set of laws.

The first essential law of Gestalt psychology is that the brain seeks to "fill in the gaps" when only part of an experience is presented. This generative process of perception is called "reification" and is applied to all sensory experiences: to what we see, hear, touch, and feel. In Figure 4.1, the object is incomplete; however, we recognize it for what it is by "filling in" the details. We do this by integrating something experienced now with something previously experienced. It is a process known as "*totality*", where conscious experience is considered globally or as a whole.

FIGURE 4.1 Totality *(Source: https://www. smashingmagazine. com/2014/03/design- principles-visual- perception-and-the- principles-of-gestalt/)*

A second law of Gestalt psychology is the law of *"proximity"*, asserting that experiences close in similarity are attached meaning as a singular whole instead of separately. An example of this is how we learn to read or play music. The letters and musical notes make little sense on their own but are essential in understanding the larger experience of reading words or of playing music. The story or song, when mapped together with letters, words, and notes, provides a way of making meaning through the use of patterns, linking one set of experiences previously known to something larger in the present experience. This is consistent with the earlier work of Bertrand Russell (1913) on his theory of logical types. He indicated that in order to establish a class, a shift is needed to understand a collection of objects (i.e., a group of chairs to the concept of furniture). Piaget (1970) applied these precepts to examine the processes associated with cognitive development. He focused on "whole structures" of knowledge and qualitatively researched the development of learning. Within his theory, Piaget viewed the basis of learning as discovery or a reconstruction by rediscovery, not simply repetition. Although you will hear more about Piaget's contributions, it is enough to say that he was influenced by the assumptions of Gestalt psychology to the process of cognitive growth and learning. These assumptions are:

- *Meaningful inquiry:* Gestalt theory implies that experiences, especially those associated with varying degrees of trauma, are fragmented. They contain gaps and elements that do not exactly fit into a larger picture for understanding. By placing alongside the sensory elements of an experience while providing a safe context to be explored in the present, the natural inclination of the brain to piece together the parts will ensue. Vygotsky (1978) described this as the *zone of proximal development*, which implies that the gap between what is known and what is possible to know is where meaningful learning occurs.

- *Meaningful application:* Gestalt learning theory contends that when people come across information or concepts that are fragmented or chaotic, the mind seeks to organize them in an attempt to both recognize and apply the emergent meanings. This view of learning is reminiscent of Frankl's (1949) contention that adversity gives rise to life course corrections. The emergence of wisdom comes not from running from the fire but by withstanding the heat long enough to consider what the fire represents. Although counterintuitive, most people mention periods of crisis first when asked, "What moments in life did you learn the most about yourself?"

- *Holistic learning:* When individuals experience life holistically, incorporating multiple sensory inputs as well as past and present experiences, they can perceive, think about, and act upon a new concept in its entirety rather than seeking to understand each part separately as if broken off from each other. Bruner (1960) referenced this as placing experience into learning "structures" that aid in the transfer of principles and ideas to life's other areas, where learning structures are themselves intertwined with each other. He noted:

  The teaching and learning of structure, rather than simply the mastery of facts and techniques, is at the center of the classic problem of transfer. ... If earlier learning is to render later learning easier, it must do so by providing a general picture in terms of which the relations between things encountered earlier and later are made as clear as possible. (Bruner, 1973, p. 12)

According to Piaget (1954), the learner travels through stages in which they accept ideas they may later discard as wrong. Furthermore, he viewed this construction of understanding through the active participation of two processes especially applicable to adult development (Piaget, 1973). The first process is the term *scheme*. Piaget (1970) defined this as a pattern of stimuli and movements that activate as a whole. A scheme represented a "gestalt with a history." It embodies past experience, generalizing and differentiating to varying contexts in varying ways. As Piaget (1954) envisioned this, a child's existing schema must make accommodations to allow for and include new information. For example, when a child learns that white granular substance tastes sweet and good, then later encounters salt for the first time (and takes a big taste!), they may have a very different experience. They might become confused, upset, and will try it again and again until they are able to accept a class of white granular substances that are not sweet. Piaget also described in detail the child's revolving or spiraling process for assimilating information from the immediate environment through the sensorimotor system. This evolved, over time, into the child's motor skills, the acquisition and use of language, consciousness, and the perception of reality.

Alfred Adler (1927) decades earlier had suggested that dividing a person into parts (i.e., preconscious, conscious, and unconscious) or forces (i.e., id, ego, superego) was mechanistic and missed the essence of people. As a central aspect of his counseling approach, Adler believed that understanding the whole person was qualitatively different that just understanding the parts of someone. He also voiced the early foundations of existentialism where life has only the meaning we ascribe to it, where our senses do not see the world but rather apprehends it (Adler, 1937/1964). Again, as if signaling the way toward resilience, he believed that life was, by definition, challenging. Living could be eased by forming friendships, establishing intimacy beyond sexual stereotypes, contributing to society beyond self-interest, and living life with courage, or a willingness to act regardless of the perceived dangers. This is not bravery or the absence of fear but a *readiness to accept the absence of guarantees* while moving forward on a path uniquely their own.

An Openness to Dissonance

This growth process is framed in how individuals address the inherent dissonance created when seeking to make sense of novel information or experiences. An individual can either integrate the "novel" (Rotter, 1954) or new experience to their previous learning scheme or they can change the quality of that scheme to "accommodate" the essence of the new learning structure. Selman (1980) contended that people fit new experiences into previous schemata's (assimilation) while also "discovering" new learning structures (accommodation) to retain stability. Piaget (1954) suggested that assimilation and accommodation are active processes that at times oppose each other and also complement each other. Though likely true for all of us, new information often disrupts established ideas and concepts of what is real and what is not, resulting in a collision of old and new. These collisions are disruptive and create disequilibrium where in order to incorporate challenging experiences (emotional, cognitive, or behaviors), a loosening from previous learning structures is required. The current "waking up" of White America to racial injustice is a social example of this collision. When new, conflicting information is indisputably presented to the status quo, people are confronted with a choice to resolve the conflict by modifying or creating new ideas, categories, and concepts that allow a synthesis of the conflict into a new understanding (or neural pathways).

It is an *equilibration* process, triggered by dissonant experiences, where in finding a new balance, something new emerges.

Mezirow's (1991) work on critical reflection affirms that individuals, in confronting environmental demands, use their reflective systems to make meaning. He asserted that within unfamiliar situations, individuals "create" new meaning schemes that make sense of divergent experiences. Kohlberg and Mayer (1971) illustrated this same learning process in their progressive view of education. They advocated developing a learning environment that presented graded series of experiences to stimulate growth for both assimilation and accommodation. From this perspective, learning is not about teaching but about supplying the necessary conditions for development when confronted with increasing levels of ambiguity. The zone of proximal development is entered when learners are both supported and "stretched" to make new connections when confronted with conflicting experiences or uncertainty, leading to the emergence of new learning structures (schemes). It is this willingness to consider the possibility of something else, to look for connections in contrast to previous learning experiences, that Vygotsky contended led to higher level thinking. Systems theorists refer to this as *morphogenesis*, whereby a family reacts to a perceived change by "moving away" from its status quo (Hoffman, 1981). In response to new information, roles, or expectations, a family is stretched to become qualitatively different. Interdependently then, all members grow.

Activity: Unique Outcomes

The questions below elicit efforts that highlight unseen strengths and introduce the idea that problems are not always occurring (exceptions) and provide a window into future "ways of being" (see Table 4.1). It further guides well-meaning counselors away from the temptation to judge or blame clients for their difficulties and encourages a mutual remembering to the better moments in a person's lived experience.

TABLE 4.1 Remembering Unique Efforts

What is <u>different</u> about you in those moments when the struggle or concern has less of a hold on you?
What do you have more <u>access</u> to in yourself in moments that feel "more on track"? What is your best guess about how this happens for you?
How do you keep the struggle or concern at bay when you <u>need to</u>? What are you more focused on during those times?
As you come to terms with your current struggle, <u>who</u> is in your corner, and what might they whisper in your ear?

Adapted from White & Epson (1990)

Even in the bleakest circumstances, resources, strengths, and exceptions to the problem pattern can be gleaned through a conversation of daily events where the smallest details can contradict perceptions of defeat and hopelessness. With a learning partner or individually with pen in hand, consider a current life struggle and reflect on the questions above. They are designed to remember those moments of resilient efforts that have been forgotten in the wake of your current struggle. Following each remembering, be sure to push yourself by asking, "And what else was different?"

For individuals and systems, although there is a natural drive toward homeostasis, it only engages during times of dissonance. Piaget (1954) referred to this as the power of disequilibrium, while Festinger (1962) contended that when a person encounters information that directly contradicts their concept about a given subject, they will either change their behavior or change their concept (perception) to accommodate the new information. These concepts of equilibration and cognitive dissonance have a direct impact on our capacity to be empathetic to others, both positively and negatively, depending on which way the accommodation goes in a relational context. If the relationship is open to new information and conflict, then the forces for change and renewal are stimulated; otherwise, as a closed system, it declines into entropy. Davis (1976) distinguished open from closed systems by explaining:

> Closed systems are totally isolated from and independent of their environment; they are static, predictable, and ultimately tend towards a state of equilibrium, stillness, inactivity. An open system is defined as an exchange of matter with its environment, importing and exporting energy, building up and breaking down its own component parts. (p. 281)

Status quo stifles innovation and denies creativity a place to thrive. Only disruption can provide the elements for growth and renewal.

When counselors accentuate discrepancies, anxiety surfaces, but often so does an awareness of choice. Mousavi and Gigerenzer (2014) noted that uncertainty had beneficial decision-making outcomes, where an awareness of mixed feelings and experiences leads toward a motivation for resolving inner incongruities. Miller and Rollnick (2002), in their seminal work on the tenets of motivational interviewing (MI), described this sense of ambivalence as a central experience to be explored and resolved when discussing behavior changes with clients. They normalized ambivalence as a reasonable emotional and cognitive state when balancing "the need to do something different" with the benefits of the "status quo." Anyone who has sought to change an aspect of their lifestyle (e.g., smoking, weight loss, exercise) knows this inner dialogue well. It is not the absence of ambivalence that embodies motivation but the presence of it. The MI counselor utilizes a strong empathic relationship devoid of preconceived clinical goals so that the advantages and disadvantages of the problematic behavior as well as the advantages and disadvantages of changing are openly considered.

The natural proclivity for seeking balance in the face of disequilibrium or dissonance is contingent on staying open to life's unpredictability and unforeseen challenges, challenges that are opportunities to grow in surprising and meaningful ways. The mind's most natural state is an attunement to the moment. It seeks closure when presented with fragmented experiences and develops new neural pathways when the PNS is activated to assist with tolerating the dissonance required for transformative understanding. This openness is an essential characteristic of empathic counseling relationships. Bugenthal (1987) contended that counselors "need only to begin" to "enter the encounter without concern about its exact nature or outcome" (p. 90). It highlights a trust in the self-healing properties of others and a commitment to the transformative energy of dissonance and equilibration.

There is a story of a man who, upon finding an emperor moth struggling to force itself through a small hole, kindly cut away the cocoon to ease the emergence of the moth. What he failed to realize in his haste to be helpful was how the struggle to free itself from the cocoon provided the moth needed fluids to be forced into its wings. Only then would the moth be prepared to fly. Without the struggle, as the man witnessed, the moth would never be able to fly. So, it is with resilience-centered counseling. Appreciating how individuals have been "stretched" by life's struggles allows a window into those resilient attributes necessary in one's fight for personal freedom. If you believe that we find in others what we believe to be true for ourselves, then if you have faith in the unique and surprising resources of people as they confront the often-insurmountable odds to a better life, you will find such ... together. It is not the absence of suffering that equates to better living but the ability to reflect in such a way that something new emerges. When this happens, it is often familiar, sometimes surprising, but always meaningful in two essential ways: (a) how you see the parts of yourself defines who you are becoming, b) and how you see the parts of your history provides wisdom about the relationships around you.

Top Takeaways

1. People inherently seek patterns and connections between the parts of what they perceive. Gestalt psychology arose from such a paradigm and contended that cognitive growth occurs through meaningful inquiry, meaningful application, and holistic learning.

2. All learning is characterized by the experience and transformation of dissonant life experiences that provide the revision of cognitive structures in adapting to novel experiences

3. Though likely true for all of us, new information often disrupts established ideas and concepts of what is real and what is not, resulting in a collision of old and new. These collisions are disruptive and create disequilibrium where in order to incorporate challenging experiences (emotional, cognitive, or behaviors), a loosening from previous learning structures is required.

4. When learners are both supported and "stretched" to make new connections when confronted with conflicting experiences or uncertainty, new learning structures (schemes) emerge.

5. The mind's most natural state is an attunement to the moment. It seeks closure when presented with fragmented experiences and develops new neural pathways when the PNS is activated to assist with tolerating the dissonance required for transformative understanding. This openness is an essential characteristic of empathic counseling relationships.

Second- and Third-Order Change

Something in people's attempted "solutions," the very ways they are trying to alter a problem, contributes most to the problem's maintenance or exacerbation. ... Problems begin from some ordinary life difficulty, of which there is never any shortage. ... But for a difficulty to turn into a problem, only two conditions need be fulfilled: (1) the difficulty is mishandled, and (2) when the difficulty is not resolved, more of the same "solution" is applied ... Then the original difficulty will be escalated, by a vicious-cycle process ... into a problem whose eventual size and nature may have little apparent similarity to the original difficulty.

—*Fisch et al. (1982, pp. 13–14)*

History has a way of creating amazing convergences. During World War II the Allies put together think tanks of different academics to muster intellectual and technological prowess in an effort to defeat the Axis powers of Germany, Japan, and Italy. The work of Bertrand Russell and Alfred Whitehead (1913/1962) on the Law of Logical Types was integrated into the work from the think tanks and the work of Ludwig von Bertalanffy (1968), which gave rise to general system theories. Family therapists commandeered these ideas and others in the 1950s and 1960s to develop a new way of conceptualizing psychopathology in the context of a family system. These approaches tended to minimize or ignore any notions concerning mental disease or disorder and directed attention to what was occurring in the context of familial relationships. In the late 1940s anthropologist Gregory Bateson translated the ideas and principles of general systems theory, or what some called "cybernetics," to the behavioral sciences. *Cybernetics* is the study of self-regulating systems in nature. Bateson joined a team at the Mental Research Institute (MRI) that was established by Don Jackson in 1959. Bateson focused his work on feedback loops in communication that occur on multiple levels, and he helped define the idea of cybernetics with his then spouse Margaret Mead. They rejected the long-held belief in science (i.e., naive realism) whereby an independent observer is somehow separate from what is being observed (Ross, 1977). In contrast to more empirical approaches where truth is fundamentally singular and objectively verifiable (D'Andrea, 2000), Bateson suggested that the observer is part of the system being observed as soon as the observation commences. This idea of second-order cybernetics asserts that both the observer and the observed regulate and change each other. They are, by definition, interdependent.

This is the general contention of the self-in-relation theory proposed by Surrey (1991) where individual growth occurs within meaningful relationships. The capacity to form deep, mutually empathic relationships provides purpose and meaning in one's life. In essence, we need others, and others need us; and more than that, these relationships shape both our view of ourselves and of others. Comb's (1954) early theory on perception explained that "how a person behaves will be a direct outgrowth of the perceptions existing at any moment" (p. 65) and are constantly in a state of revision influenced by interaction with others, culture, and society at large. The interdependency between people and the influence relationships can have on an individual's worldview and perception of self-worth highlights another step away from the counselor as expert and outside arbiter of reality and toward one that (a) acknowledges the experiences of others as real and b) co-constructs meaning within this accepting relationship. The following are theoretical intentions that can assist counselors when seeking this kind of relationship with othes.

Marshaling Our Resources

While working with MRI, Bateson became keenly interested in the work of Milton Erickson, an atheoretical psychiatrist who was using hypnosis as a therapeutic intervention with reportedly great effect in the 1950s and 1960s (Haley, 1987). Bateson and Mead had previously contacted Erickson to consult about trance-like experiences they were observing in their research on tribal people. Bateson spent significant time at MRI conducting studies on therapeutic communication in an effort to sort out the differences between what works in talk therapy and what might not. Erickson was the subject of many of those studies. Erickson refused to name his model, though consistent statements he made over time allowed those who studied under him and with him to make assumptions about his approach to therapy. He pioneered the use of hypnosis and indirect suggestion in psychotherapy to assist clients in marshaling their resources to work in their benefit as opposed to working at odds with their interests (O'Hanlon, 1987).

Erikson repeatedly asserted that the client brings with them what they need to find relief. The role of the therapist was to identify what was already known but perhaps forgotten or misapplied and help clients utilize their strengths and wisdom with increased intentionality. He stepped into the worldview of the client, let go of his own view of truth for the client, and accepted what they were thinking, saying, and doing in relation to their problems without suggesting they stop what they are doing or do something else. This idea became known as the *utilization principle* (O'Hanlon, 1987; Rossi, 1980). By not challenging the emotionally charged part of their lives, resistance was minimized, engagement with the counselor maximized, and a willingness of clients to consider other ways of interacting was facilitated (Dagirmanjian et al., 2007). Erickson's focus was on the client's theory about what the problem and solution might be (Bertolino & O'Hanlon, 2002). His methods and work influenced many of the family therapy, brief therapy, and later postmodern practitioners (Rossi, 1980; O'Hanlon, 1987).

Influenced by Erickson's work, the Mental Research Institute (MRI) developed what they called "problem oriented therapy" and limited themselves to 10 sessions in order to solve a given problem, which was defined in the family's or client's terms (Watzlawick et al., 1974; Weakland et al., 1974). They sidelined diagnosis as problematic as well as an exploration to the "why" of problematic interactions. They viewed all actions or "symptoms" as efforts to solve their problems or as the consequence of mishandling ordinary life challenges. These "unfortunate solutions" maintained the problem, where life became "just one damn thing after another" (Watzlawick et al., 1974). They suggested that in fact life is just one damn thing after another and often problems arise when life descends into the same damn thing every day. Therefore, the goal of therapy becomes shifting back to one damn thing after another. They saw these initial attempts at solving their life problems as first-order change and believed a second-order change was needed so that problems might resolve themselves. This was accomplished by shifting the relationship people had with their problems. Either the cycle of interaction was interrupted on a suggestion by the therapist or the "frame" of the problem maintaining the problematic behavior was altered or reframed back to the family.

They suggested that first-order change often fails to produce the desired results for people. Simply making a decision to stop doing something without something else to do is largely ineffective and requires dedication and stamina across vast amounts of time that people were not generally inclined to invest and/or maintain. Counseling focused on merely the absence of the problem and did little or nothing to change the rules that govern the system surrounding and supporting the problem. Counseling was viewed as ineffective in promoting lasting change.

A Shift Is Needed

In much the same way that insomnia is maintained the more the experience of not sleeping is focused on, so are the family's effort to solve systemic problems. They are functional in securing equilibrium to the system and provide an uncomfortable sacrifice in order to keep things the same. Satir (1998) contended that when balance is maintained through inappropriate roles, restrictive rules, and/or unrealistic expectations, needs will not be met in family relationships and dysfunction occurs. She contended that when this cycle begins, self-esteem in each member is lowered and defensive behavior with one another increases. As with the MRI, a shift away from the observable problems was needed and a focus on the roles, interactions, and rules that governed the problem was required. In contrast to the first-order change emphasis of empirical models, a focus on a second-order change was needed to encourage more open, positive feedback loops between people and their relationship with the problem behavior and interactions. This perspective required counselors to focus on the "space between" people. This is an orientation that understands that most problems are far more complex and contextual, requiring more than merely finding the missing piece of a puzzle. The following are brief examples that seek to illustrate the shift to a second-order mindset.

Shifting the Rules

Stemming from how Erickson would step inside the internal worldview, or frame, of another's experience and provide subtle shifts allowing for small degrees of increased freedom from the problem or symptoms, the term "reframing" was introduced by the MRI in their book *Change* and was defined as a way "to change the conceptual and/or emotional setting in which a situation is experienced and to place it in another frame which fit the 'facts' of the same concrete situation equally well or even better, and thereby changes its entire meaning" (Watzlawick et al., 1974, p. 95). It is the strategic use of language to elicit new meanings, expand perspectives, and acknowledge strengths and patterns of resilience while highlighting people's choices. It also creates an assumption of accountability rather than blame or determinism.

As Bertolino and O'Hanlon (2002) articulated, "If the person is not the problem, but has a certain relationship to the problem, then the relationship can change. ... If the problem is trying to recruit a client, he or she can refuse to join" (p. 133). This is not to be confused with merely wishing away problems or creating new fictions. The intent of reframing is to shed light on the resources available to clients made unknown by the constricting repetition of the problem cycle.

The Milan group (Bosocolo et al., 1987) contended that all problems have a positive connotation. This might be a mother complaining of how she is treated by her children while sacrificing her own needs so that her children will "need for nothing," a taskmaster father that is willing to be hated by his children so that they are prepared to handle the difficulty of life that awaits them, a spouse that keeps things inside to protect and save their partner from their burdens, or a teenager that acts out as a way to communicate an unmet need for belonging, honesty, and/or independence. A submissive mother, a rigid father, a secretive spouse, and rebellious teenagers are not just problem behaviors but also well-intended interactions that have unspoken and, more often than not, benevolent meanings.

An Example

Early in my (Colin) career as a family counselor, I had developed close ties with school counselors across an array of regional school districts. As a former special educator, and like my colleagues, I had an appreciation for how the psychosocial histories of my students were far more influential to their learning than the lessons I presented. It was this curiosity that led me to the counseling field, and I quickly garnered a reputation for being able to work with the "tough" adolescent cases. One such referral was 17-year-old, White, cisgender female student. The school counselor indicated that she was at risk of being expelled due to her ever-mounting absences and the impact this was having on her academic record. They had been unable to convince the student or the parent (a single mother) of the severity of the situation. The school counselor was worried, and although she found the student respectful, her quiet nature made it difficult to know much else. School officials began to see her absences as defiant and likely incorrigible. Since my office was just down the street from the high school, we agreed that she would be provided an off-campus pass to see me.

We did not initially discuss her absences but instead focused on who she was, what she was like, and what interested her the most. We agreed to meet once or twice a week with the request that she consider inviting her mother to join us for a session, if and when she considered this to be helpful in our work together. I learned she was the oldest of three children, who all lived with their mother and ailing grandmother. Their father had died earlier in a farming accident, and due to financial constraints, they had moved from their home in the country, where each had their own bedroom, into a downtown three-bedroom apartment. Her mother had found a position as a nurse's aide where her work hours varied week to week. When her mother finally joined us, she spoke lovingly of her daughter and the care she provided to her siblings and grandmother. She made it clear that given her unpredictable schedule, she needed her daughter "to take care of things" when she was not able. Her daughter, my client, did this without question.

I asked the school counselor to arrange a meeting with the relevant school officials and teachers and, with permission from the mother and student, shared the following:

> On the surface of things, the chronicity of her absences might suggest someone who
> was irresponsible and uncaring. If you looked only at her academic record, you might

(Continued)

conclude she lacked motivation and was indifferent to her education. She was referred to me with these concerns in mind. From the moment I met this young woman, I found just the opposite to be true. In light of the tragic loss of their father, and the impact this had on her family, she demonstrated unwavering loyalty. She has been willing to sacrifice her own education, which she so badly desires for herself, in order to provide the care needed by her siblings and grandmother while her mother is away working. It is her strong sense of responsibility and devotion that keeps her from school; and on those days she is able to attend, she does so with the anxiety and fear a parent might have when leaving her children to care for themselves. It is an unfair expectation, and yet she does not complain. She talks glowingly of her family with the deep belief that they will all find their way through this. She is proud of her mother, and although she worries about them, she is thankful she can be of use, a use she believes keeps them all together. Her absences are not about defiance, but of love. The question, I believe, is not whether you should remove this student from school, but how the school and county can find a way to support this family so that this student does not have to make the unfathomable choice between her education and caring for her family?

A way was found, and she eventually graduated from high school and became a first-generation college student at a regional institution.

Shifting the Interaction

As noted above, the Milan group began in the late 1960s and early 1970s synthesizing the ideas of Selvina Palazzoli, Luigi Boscolo, Gianfranco Cecchin, and Guiliana Prata. They expanded on the interdependency of members around a presenting problem, as noted in Bateson's cybernetic theory, and blended the strategic techniques as noted from the MRI group into a unique variety of what has been called "ultrastrategic" (Nichols & Schwartz, 1998, p. 374). They published *Paradox and Counterparadox* in 1978 and introduced the ideas of viewing the symptoms people bring to counseling as positive connotations. They made heavy use of rituals designed to activate the family to run counter to rigid family rules or to exaggerate them. This "prescribing of the symptom" was central to how both the MRI and Milan group sought to interrupt the influence the problem had on systemic functioning. This technique sought to empower others by having them decide when, where, and how to focus on their symptoms. The emphasis on second-order change, assisting others to attune rather than avoid or judge regarding their relationship with problematic symptoms, was essential and intentional.

Prescribing the Symptom

In prescribing the symptom, for example, a counselor might encourage a client to schedule a time in the day that might give the symptom (e.g., worry, regret, sadness) the full attention it deserves. The client is instructed to use this limited time (e.g., 45 minutes) to make note of only that which they are struggling against and to keep track of their experience in any way that is most helpful (e.g., note taking, prayer, mediation) and report on this in their next meeting. If the symptoms appear either before or after this time, the client is instructed to put the troublesome thoughts and feelings aside with the knowledge there is a designated block of time to give it their undivided attention. This shows that by providing clients increased freedom to dictate when, where, and how often the presenting symptoms are consciously addressed, the experience of the symptoms as uncontrollable spontaneous invasions shifts to one of deliberate distress chosen by the client. By focusing attention on that which was being avoided, mishandled, or distorted, the client was provided space to assert agency over the symptoms—a "rebellion" against the influence of oppressive symptoms and internal narratives.

In addition to shifting the interaction between an individual and the problem itself, interrupting the interaction between family members can also be encouraged, if the family system has the capacity to do so. Jay Haley, who was a research associate at MRI, helped found their Brief Therapy Institute, which provided resources and extended training for Virginia Satir, Salvador Minuchin, Cloe Madanas, and others—all key figures in experiential, structural, and strategic family therapy. Family therapy, as developed by these clinicians, situated problems as residing between family members or embedded in relationships. These relationships served the purpose of maintaining or returning the family to homeostasis. Strategic family therapists were initially concerned with taking a direct approach and giving the therapist responsibility for change. Structural family therapists, like Munichin, were concerned with structures of authority within a family and establishing boundaries between and within generations. Their interventions were designed to create dissonance to invoke change. Pattern disruption, restructuring, and repositioning members of the family became the primary focus of therapy (Haley, 1987; Satir, 1984; Munichin, 1974; Madanas, 1981). A wonderful example of this was developed by Mara Selvini-Palazzoli (1986) in her strategic work with families. She would prescribe a universal directive designed to interrupt "family games" by strengthening the parental alliance. Entitled an "invariable prescription," she would meet alone with the parents and instruct them to keep everything talked about in session a secret, explore ways to leave the children without explaining their absence, and separately track the behaviors of all family members. To the surprise of parents, by breaking up the family games, the children's symptomatic behaviors improved (Diller, 2000).

Example

While working at my (Bill) very first practicum site as a student in the late 1990s, I had a young man come see me with an older cousin who had taken him in after he left his family with a list of complaints about how he was being mistreated. Ellis was a straight-A student who worked part-time and full-time jobs to save for college all through high school. Now as a senior in high school, he had had enough of his parents sequestering his hard-earned money and refusing to allow him access to it for some leisure activities or for a date with a girl who had caught his eye. His cousin was very sympathetic and at the same time heartbroken by what was happening to the family. The list of complaints was very long, and after the first session, I suggested to Ellis that he make a list of them and put them in some sort of priority order so we might take them on one at a time. It became clear that Ellis really valued his family by the investment he had made in precisely

(Continued)

identifying what he thought the problems were and the energy behind his efforts to solve them. Ellis thought this was a good idea and went to work.

He returned 3 weeks later with a list that was approximately 40 pages long, single spaced, typed, and placed in priority order. It was quite an impressive list. He was anxious to get to work on it and felt the need to get this situation sorted out in the next few days. I looked at the list and said that it would take me a little time to read through it so that I was sure I understood precisely what was going on. Ellis became quite distressed by this and stated, "Well I was hoping to get this solved today because next weekend is the 4th of July and my family had invited me (and his cousin) on a weekend outing to a local resort for the annual family gathering and reunion. How can I go when all these problems are happening?" I was very concerned about what might happen and resisted the idea that he should go. He pushed back hard, stating that his family was important, and he has never missed a reunion in the past. I again stated my concerns about his going, indicating that it might just blow the whole thing up! Ellis became insistent, so I indicated that there was nothing I could do to stop him from going if that is what he decided. My advice was not to go, but if he decided to go, he had to make me one promise and that was to refuse to talk about anything he put on the 40-page list while he was with his family. If they wanted to have discussions about any problems, they all would have to wait for our next appointment, and we could all sit down and talk about them. Ellis agreed, and we brought his cousin into the session to clarify the rules of engagement with the family at the reunion. His cousin felt comfortable monitoring the situation and having the role of informing the family that they had sought an outside "expert" to help with the family situation and that I had instructed them to refrain from any discussion of problems until they returned from their holiday weekend. They left, and I worried and wondered how it would go … a lot.

Ellis called and left a message after the weekend indicating he had to reschedule his appointment by pushing it back a week. When he showed up with his whole family at the next appointment, they all seemed quite content with each other. Ellis came in first and told me that everything was better and that his family wanted to meet me. I invited them in, and they all started in on how much better Ellis was and thanked me for working with him to solve their problems. When they got up to leave, I asked Ellis to stay behind for a minute. I asked him what he wanted me to do about the list and he asked if I could hang on to it for safekeeping in case he needed it later. He has never contacted me about that list. It appears that when Ellis and his family took their attention away from the problems and the resulting tug of war that had developed in the family, they all simply let go of the rope and had a good time being with one another. Even though the intervention was somewhat prescriptive with a touch of paradox and placing me the therapist in the role of a trusted expert, the way it developed and resolved was quite abrupt and surprising. I did not expect it to turn out that way at all, and it pointed out clearly to me how resilient people are, especially in the context of their relationships.

Shifting the Roles

Murray Bowen, trained as a psychoanalyst, brought psychoanalytic theory to a family systems perspective in the 1960s (Nichols & Schwartz, 1998). Bowen worked at the Menninger Clinic with families who had a family member suffering from schizophrenia in the 1940s and 1950s. Bowen concluded that the family consisted of the unit of disorder, and he began treating them together (Nichols & Schwartz, 1998). He felt problems in families were situated across generations (vertical) and within generations (horizontal). Situations that encompass both aspects, or only horizontal problems, often were recognizable through *triangles,* where one person solicits the aid/support/ unwitting participation in the problem from one family member targeting another (Sharf, 1996). These recursive patterns of communication occur in response to relational conflict. When two people are in discord, a third person is triangulated in an effort to alleviate discomfort (Watzlawick et al., 1967). Recounting an observation of a family through a two-way mirror at the MRI clinic, Jay Haley noticed a discontented child sitting between two parents. Very quickly, the child would do something that annoyed the father, who would then abruptly command the child to stop the behavior. Almost immediately, the mother told the father to lower his voice and leave the child alone. After a brief pause, the cycle would repeat itself. Each played a role in these "family games" that maintained family equilibrium by taking the focus off that which was being avoided (e.g., drinking, parental discord, mental illness, trauma). Satir (1988) contended that by retaining circular and rigid communication roles, in an effort to maintain harmony, family members experience increasing isolation from one another, decreased levels of worth self-esteem, and defensive behaviors (see Table 5.1).

TABLE 5.1 Family Roles

Communication role	Sacrifice
Blamer: Fault finding and controlling	Takes focus off their own actions at the sacrifice of their intimacy with others (I'm lonely)
Placater: Apologetic and seeking approval	Reduces conflict and maintains harmony in the relationship at the sacrifice of personal needs (I'm nothing without you)
Distractor: Tangential and irrelevant	Takes attention off the hot issues in the family at the sacrifice of personal needs (Nobody cares)
Computing: Unemotional and reasonable	Aids in their emotional safety and protection at the sacrifice of having interpersonal relationships (I'm vulnerable)

In her work with families, Satir encouraged members to break out of their recursive patterns of interactions and to tolerate the relational distress long enough to ask for what they needed from one another, directly and honestly. She considered this shift to more congruent communication the goal of family counseling. Murray Bowen (1978) considered this shift a growth toward increased autonomy in relationship with others. He saw problems as embedded in the family, or at least managed through a family process. He believed that as anxiety rises within relational experiences, feelings and reactions are determined by compliance and conformity to reduce the tension. He considered the ability to differentiate from others and to manage or regulate anxiety so as to make independent decisions the primary element associated with change. In other words, the ability to hang on to oneself rather than on others, to self-regulate in the face of interpersonal dissonance, and to live in accordance to values and virtues deemed personally important was the essence of meaningful living.

Example

Many years before becoming a psychologist, I (Bill) worked in the juvenile court system in the 1970s as a diversion specialist. My job was to divert minor offenders and what we called "status offenders" away from the juvenile justice system and toward services in the community. I encountered a young man, Jason, who was skipping school and running away from home. He had a blended family that consisted of his biological younger sister, mother, and stepfather, Hank, who was a former marine. Hank was what he called "old school" when it came to discipline with the children. He would say to me repeatedly, "Spare the rod, spoil the child!" Over our brief time together, it became apparent to me that Jason had a tremendous amount of respect for his stepfather and wanted to please him but felt like this was an impossible task. It was also apparent that Hank, who cried in my office talking about the horrible fate that awaited his stepson if he continued on the path to ruin, clearly loved his stepson. Hank yelled at people, a lot: He yelled at Jason, his sister, his spouse, and even me about what he wanted, which when examined carefully was a decent life for his family. Hank made huge sacrifices for his family and was totally dedicated to them. I talked with Hank about how his yelling at people was not helpful and that I knew it was his way of saying he loved them and wanted them to do and be better. He surprised me by acknowledging this as a fact and one he felt he could not control. I suggested, not knowing what else to do, that whenever he felt like yelling, he was to put it off and yell at me instead of his family. He had to do everything he could to put off any yelling and confine it to our phone time together. Thus, every morning for the next few weeks, Hank would call me and yell at me over the phone for 10 minutes about whatever issues were confronting him about his family. Occasionally, he would call yelling at other times when things were overwhelming for him. When I answered the phone and heard him yelling at me, I just set it down so my ears would not be damaged and checked in with him every couple of minutes to see if it was helping. After a while he stayed on the phone and yelled for less and less time until our morning talks turned into talks about other ways to be an effective parent for his family. His son Jason settled down fairly quickly after testing this new way of being for his family by some minor acting out that was now handled differently than before. He found that he could please his stepfather and have it noticed because he was spending less time feeling the sting of his stepfather's harsh words prognosticating him about having a disastrous life if he kept on acting out. My suggestion was out of desperation as opposed to any real insight or skill. I lucked out, and it worked. Jason went on to complete high school and went into business with his stepfather. Changing the rules of who gets yelled at while making it okay for Hank to yell at somebody when Jason made a mistake seemed to take the pressure off of Jason for not being perfect so he could find other ways of being and doing while his stepfather was now able to connect with him in ways that were unlikely before. Life was far from perfect, and nobody was yelling about it anymore.

Third-Order Change

In second-order change, the focus shifts from doing more of the same to changing the rules that apply to the situation. Narrative therapists like David Epston (2015) have introduced another way of encouraging and maintaining change. In his work over the years with people who find themselves struggling with what has become known as feeding and eating disorders, he and others noticed that these disorders do not appear with the same frequency (and sometimes not at all) outside of Western and Western-influenced cultures. In working with clients who struggle with feeding and eating and externalizing these problems into experience near descriptions, clients began realizing and articulating the influence of the larger culture in forming and internalizing body image concepts that were unhealthy and even result in the death of the client. Clients, in working through these issues, often ended up identifying media's influence in the development of their self-concepts as not being thin enough, perfect enough, and so on. Some clients became energized to take action so others would suffer less from these cultural influences. These actions would result in letter-writing campaigns to the fashion industry, protests at fashion shows, and shining light on an industry that exploits people by repeatedly defining acceptable body image with models who were outside the ordinary in terms of size and proportion. Some clients joined together with others to engage in activism targeting changes in the fashion industry, demanding they use images that are more representative of humans across the globe in their efforts to promote their products. You may have started to see some of the results of these actions in more recent advertisements expanding the demographics of models for clothing products. These are examples of what is becoming known as third-order change. While in second-order change interventions are directed towards a given client's ecosystem and their

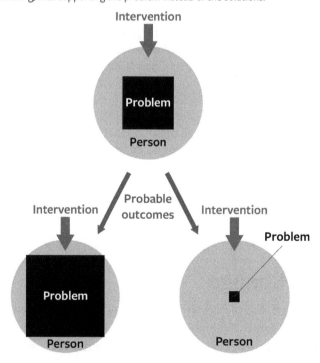

First Order Change

Problems tend to be viewed as situated within the individual. They are addressed or "solved" by and within that individual.

Interventions tend to be about increasing or decreasing the frequency of something with the goal of returning to homeostasis. This may often—though not always—be disempowering, thus supporting the problem instead of the solutions.

Change is limited to within the person.

FIGURE 5.1 First-Order Change

Second Order Change

Problems tend to be viewed as situated within the system containing the individual. They are addressed or "solved" by changing the rules under which the problems operate.

This is often done through the establishment or re-establishment of boundaries, disrupting or modifying the problem's pattern, changing the person's relationship with the problem and with the family system, or focusing on solutions and change instead of blame and treatment.

This may often—though not always—be empowering, thus supporting the solutions and the person instead of the problems.

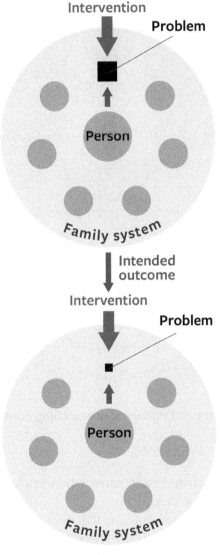

Change of change.

FIGURE 5.2 Second-Order Change

Third Order Change

Problems tend to be viewed as situated within the sociocultural context containing the individual and the family system. They are addressed or "solved" by empowering the individual to change the rules under which the problem operates.

Interventions tend to be about empowering the client to act with personal agency in order to influence the system and larger cultural context.

This is often accomplished by identifying the client's strenghths and experience. Third order change can only be accomplished by empowering the indivudal or giving back to them the power they were deprived of, thus supporting competency.

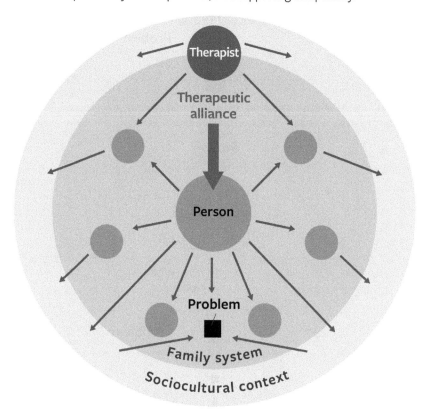

Change of changing overarching context.

FIGURE 5.3 Third-Order Change

relationship with it, third-order change interventions are often targeted toward the larger culture and the relationships people have with it.

Other examples of third-order change would include people who, after resolving traumas in their past regarding sexual abuse, become youth advocates, former gang members who commit themselves to helping others retire from gang membership, formerly incarcerated people who establish prison-to-work programs involving job training, or people forming a support group to assist others in managing or standing up to issues in their lives.

A Lingering Thought

It has been concluded that psychologists and clinicians can be so enthralled with linking presenting client symptoms to diagnostic categories that anticipation, altruism, and humor were perceived as defense mechanisms (Rashid & Ostermann, 2009). An emphasis on first-order change can blind counselors to the inherent worth of others and the insuppressible power of the human spirit. Or as Nichols and Schwartz (2001) so eloquently pointed out, "Too often clients aren't heard because therapists are doing therapy to them rather than with them" (p. 205). People are far more than the symptoms and problems they present in the counseling office. Their suffering represents resilient efforts in the face of often daunting life challenges and are reflective of relationships that constantly influence their beliefs about themselves and the world around them. The ability to listen beyond the complaints of clients and acknowledge the inherent difficulty of change is to appreciate the interdependent nature of the human experience. It is through this gaze and your relationship with with the clients that they can see, maybe for the first time, that they are not necessarily victims of their circumstances but active agents in directing their lives.

Top Takeaways

1. Cybernetics is the study of self-regulating systems in nature. In contrast to more empirical approaches where truth is fundamentally singular and objectively verifiable (D'Andrea, 2000), Bateson suggested that the observer is part of the system being observed as soon as the observation commences. This idea of second-order cybernetics asserts that both the observer and the observed regulate and change each other. They are, by definition, interdependent.

2. Milton Erickson asserted that the client brings with them what they need to find relief. The role of the therapist was to identify what was already known, but forgotten, and help clients utilize their strengths and wisdom with increased intentionality. He stepped into the worldview of the client, let go of his own view of truth for the client, and accepted what they were thinking, saying, and doing in relationship to their problems without suggesting they stop what they are doing or do something else. This idea became known as the utilization principle (O'Hanlon, 1987; Rossi, 1980).

3. Watzlawick et al. (1974) believed a second-order change was needed so that problems might resolve themselves. This was accomplished by shifting the relationship people had with their problems.

4. The term "reframing" was introduced by the MRI in their book *Change* and is defined as a way "to change the conceptual and/or emotional setting in which a situation is experienced and to place it in another frame which fit the 'facts' of the same concrete situation equally well or even better, and thereby changes its entire meaning" (Watzlawick et al., 1974, p. 95). It is the strategic use of language to elicit new meanings, expand perspectives, and acknowledge strengths and patterns of resilience while highlighting people's choices. It also creates an assumption of accountability rather than blame or determinism.

5. Strategic family therapists were initially concerned with taking a direct approach and giving the therapist responsibility for change. Structural family therapists like Munichin were concerned with structures of authority within a family and establishing boundaries between and within generations. Their interventions were designed to create dissonance to invoke change. Pattern disruption, restructuring, and repositioning members of the family became the primary focus of therapy (Haley, 1987; Satir, 1984; Munichin, 1974; Madanas, 1981).

Trauma and Resilience

When people suffering from trauma are able to stay <u>embodied</u> and <u>regulate</u> their affective states, they can tolerate small doses of suffering and pain while processing traumatic memories.

—*Sharon Stanley (2016, p. 8)*

People are not generally inclined to see a counselor, psychologist, or other mental health provider when they are feeling good. Comparatively, our interest in becoming mental health providers, at least in part, is motivated by the desire to be helpful for those not feeling well. We wish to relieve suffering. Difficulties in life resulting in what we have grown to recognize as mental health concerns have been with us throughout history. Devoting time and attention to what is going well for people has not been at the top of our list. In the 1950s, Carl Rogers and Abraham Maslow were early proponents to observe what they saw as working with people and integrated this into their fulfilment theories of human development. Humanistic psychology was born out of a reflection of sorts upon what might be going right with people in an effort to gain insight into what may be causing suffering. The effort to refocus attention away from the individual and their internal pathology to a more contextual understanding of human behavior appeared to start with the behaviorists in the mid-20th century and it was revisited by the systems theory proponents that arose in the late 1960s, 1970s, and 1980s. This systemic view allowed the profession to take a more holistic view of people and how they behave, the complexity of factors that impact client behavior, and the problems they face within the systems of which they are a part. Postmodernism embedded the client and their worldview within their context, making it imperative for counselors to view these pieces together with curiosity and humility, knowing that our own lived experiences are uniquely and naturally different from those of each client.

Learned Helplessness and Stockholm Syndrome

As has been previously noted, where we situate problems often determines how we view them and thus how we approach them. When the problem is situated inside a person, it is often viewed as a problem or pathology that is in need of remediation or removal. When the problem is situated in the person's relationships and support system, the responsibility and hence the interventions shift the focus to those relationships. When the problem is situated more broadly in the larger culture, our focus is drawn to societal and cultural change. As the field began to view clients and their problems as a part of and therefore impacted by their sociocultural systems, a research psychologist by the name of Martin Seligman was conducting experiments beginning in 1967 with dogs. These experiments entailed observing dogs and their efforts to escape painful stimuli (electric shocks) and the outcomes when escape is made temporarily impossible. After some time in the no-escape situation, the dogs appeared to give up any effort to escape and began to simply tolerate what they have been conditioned to perceive as inevitable. Even after the dogs were given the opportunity to escape the electrical shocks, they remained in the adverse environment. These experiments cast a light on what they termed "learned helplessness" (Maier & Seligman, 1967). Individuals, when no other options appear available, often just appear to do the same and to choose to remain in adverse and even torturous circumstances long after escape becomes possible and even encouraged.

As unlikely as it was, this research sparked a revolution in positive psychological thinking and research. Seligman became interested in what purpose might be served in remaining a prisoner when freedom is just an unfettered step or two away. What traits are being expressed that make the impulse to stay in pain appear imperative over pain relief? How is it helpful? Questions like these tend to lead down a path to discovering what might be in it for the individual. Is it about reinforcement schedules? A deep-seated death wish? Masochism? Self-hatred? Or *survival*? How could something that we see as so wrong, like remaining in an abusive and dangerous relationship, appear to a person to be their only viable option? How can they feel any agency when also working in cooperation with the aggressor?

Adding to the confusion, in August 1973 two bank robbers took four bank employees hostage at a bank in Stockholm, Sweden, in what turned into a 6-day standoff with the police. Over the course of those 6 days, the hostages began cooperating and even protecting the bank robbers, pleading with the police not to hurt them once they were apprehended. This was not the first time such a phenomenon has happened in our history, but it was one of the first times that it caught the fascination of the public imagination, and the term "Stockholm syndrome" was coined. Another case hit the headlines the next year involving Patty Hearst, an heir to the Hearst newspaper conglomerate, who after being taken hostage began cooperating with her captors and subsequently participated in a series of bank robberies. Perhaps one option in gaining some agency in a helpless or hopeless situation is simply cooperating with the aggressors. Domestic violence situations have long haunted and puzzled law enforcement personnel, psychologists, and counselors. The same questions appear to surface in these situations. "Why stay?" is the simplistic question that often shows up in our minds. Upon closer examination, it turns out that an abused spouse is several times more likely to be murdered after leaving a domestic violence situation than if they simply remain and tolerate the abuse. Seligman's early work pointed us in the direction we needed to look to solve this conundrum.

Posttraumatic Stress Disorder and Posttraumatic Growth

In the background of these events, the Vietnam War was ending and the phenomena of aberrant behavior in veterans was catching the eye of helping professionals. The term "posttraumatic stress syndrome" emerged in the media as an effort to explain some of the behaviors that were appearing consistently in war veterans. In past wars, these outcomes were described as "shell shock" in WWI and "neurosis of war" in WWII (van der Kolk, 2014). Though the notion that past experiences could result in psychopathology was not new, these iterations appeared to conflict with the disease model of mental illness. The bio-basis of behavior and the connections between experience and biology were not (and perhaps are still not) fully understood. The clinical interaction between what is wrong with a person and what happened to a person garnered more focus in the 1980s and 1990s. The diagnosis of posttraumatic stress disorder was officially introduced in *DSM-III* in 1980, and 7 years later, the self-defeating personality disorder (APA, 1987) was proposed to help explain why people remain in adverse and even dangerous circumstances as opposed to leaving. Once again, the tendency was to blame the person for the behavior without a clear contextual understanding of the demand characteristics present in an individual's local and larger culture. Feminist psychologists took issue with this approach to diagnosing and pathologizing people for engaging in behaviors that enhanced their survival and successfully fought to keep this diagnosis out of *DSM-IV* in 1994 (Laura Brown, personal communication, September 2001).

Further research has brought a clearer focus to the understanding of the impact of trauma on psychological health. Van der Kolk et al. (1996) suggested:

> Psychiatry as a profession has had a very troubled relationship with the idea that reality can profoundly and permanently alter people's psychology and biology. Psychiatry itself has periodically suffered from marked amnesias in which well-established knowledge has been abruptly forgotten, and the psychological impact of overwhelming experiences has been ascribed to constitutional or intrapsychic factors alone. Mirroring and intrusions, confusion, and disbelief of victims whose lives are suddenly shattered by traumatic experiences, the psychiatric profession has gone through periods of fascination with trauma, followed by periods of stubborn disbelief about the relevance of patients' stories. (p. 47)

This controversy suggested that experiences were being recognized as capable of causing psychopathology. The boundary between what we have traditionally called "mental disease" and what is simply an understandable outcome of events merged.

At the start of this century, one area of trauma research gaining more attention was the study of resiliency. Researchers sought to understand how those factors, innate or acquired, allow an individual to avoid disorder after trauma exposure, at least in the clinical sense of meeting criteria for PTSD (Bonanno, 2004). What constitutional characteristics within individuals and/or situations allowed some people to experience horrific and often multiple traumatic events while remaining relatively symptom free? Several studies of emergency services personnel suggested that contextual factors such as social, organizational, occupational, and other external support systems play a significant role in building and maintaining resilience (Hart et al., 1995; Regehr et al., 2002; Haslam & Mallon, 2003; Cowman et al., 2004; Brough, 2004). While other research suggested that a lack of empathy with victims may mitigate the impact of traumatic events (Regehr et al., 2002; Mesut et al., 2005).

Another area of inquiry of first responders was the nature of resiliency factors that could be added, regardless of individual traits or vulnerabilities, to enhance a more healthful response to traumatic events. An early study attempted to determine if training would enhance resilience in disaster workers. Paton (1994) assessed two groups of disaster workers and found that firefighters demonstrated more trauma symptoms than specifically trained disaster volunteers from varied backgrounds after engaging in search-and-rescue work for an Armenian earthquake. The author concluded that when a disaster event presents situations to rescue workers that are different enough from their routine, challenges to their traditional experience and training may arise and make it more difficult to cope (Paton, 1994). The study did not report what specific training the group of firefighters had obtained as a part of their normal duty preparation, but it did specify the volunteer training that occurred just before departure for the disaster site. The study failed to account for what sorts of traumatic experiences the firefighters may have endured before leaving for the disaster, how long the firefighters had been on the job before leaving, and additional disasters the firefighters had worked in the past. Nonetheless, the findings do suggest that preparation prior to contending with disaster events may be beneficial for people in occupations that place them in frequent contact with horrific events. Training regarding a specific type of work may help in establishing an appropriate context and expectation set that may enhance competency, thereby reducing the impact of stress. It should also be noted that Paton (1994) reported that nearly 25% of the volunteer sample (n=21) were also firefighters. This study appears to show us that the importance of specific training in mitigating the impact of traumatic stress may be crucial, especially when it occurs in close proximity to the situations for which the training is designed to address.

Contextual factors as resiliency factors also appeared in a robust study conducted by Hart et al. in 1995 in Australia, suggesting that police work may in fact have lower psychological stress than that of teachers or other nonpolice occupations (Hart et al., 1995). They proposed a four-factor interactive model for evaluating occupational stress. This consisted of "Organizational Hassles, Operational Hassles, Operational Uplifts, and Organizational Uplifts" (Hart et al., 1995, p. 142). *Organizational Hassles* are a function of seven dimensions consisting of communication, administration, supervision, ratings, coworkers, morale, and workload. Frustration, external (other operations and organizations), victims, activity, complaints, and danger drive *Operational Hassles*. *Operational Uplifts* are derived from offenders (making arrests), victims (advocating and protecting). *Organizational Uplifts* consist of the level of decision-making authority, workload (accomplishments), coworkers (support), administration (efficiency), amenities (rewards, privileges), and supervision (organizational support and caring). The study was part of a longitudinal inquiry into police stress and well-being and selected a sample of 330 police officers from the Victoria, Australia, police department in 1988 and a similar sample of 372 officers from the same department in 1990. The samples had six "perceived quality of life indicators" (Hart et al., 1995, p. 137) administered to them. They were also given the Police Daily Hassles and Uplift Scales, the Coping Response Inventory, and the NEO Personality Inventory. Aside from concluding that police officers tend to suffer less psychological distress than most other occupations, Hart et al. (1995) also concluded organizational factors have a far greater impact on an officer's well-being and stress levels than do operational factors. This conclusion indicated that the context and related local culture defined by the organization are more important to the psychological health of police officers than the type of work and experiences that are operationally endured.

Trauma Reenactment as Resiliency

This research leads one to the notion that resiliency may not be something entirely attributable to innate biological or acquired traits. It may in fact be generated and moderated by external factors and dynamic processes that are in perpetual motion, being acquired, used, and perhaps discarded when they are no longer needed. Ideas about traumatic reenactment when viewed from the lens of resiliency begins to take on a different appearance and etiology. When one experiences any event or series of events, information is obtained from the experience and put to future use. Early descriptions of reenactment were described and identified as transference phenomena and then countertransference by the likes of Freud and others (Ellenberger, 1970). These ideas appear to have morphed into an entire school of psychotherapy called *object relations* where nearly all behavior is viewed as the result of relationships to early caretakers that are repeatedly enacted, reenacted, and modified over time into what we have grown accustomed to calling a "personality." Much of the focus of these clinicians was paid to the aberrant behaviors that emerged and then tracing them back to their origins in an effort to modify the reenactment and the behavior that results into something more functional. Some have referred to these epiphanies as "corrective emotional experiences" (Yalom, 2005) and see them as essential in the psychotherapeutic process.

Could it be that reenactments are simply attempts to solve problems or even a growth pattern involved in human development? It has been suggested over the years that traumatic reenactments are simply failed attempts to have a "do over" in an effort to make the outcome different. Hence, victims of prolonged sexual abuse may act out in sexually promiscuous or inhibited ways as an effort to make what happened okay or to successfully avoid the abuse in the present. Similar patterns have been observed in childhood victims of physical abuse as well. The circumstances that stand out are the ones that do not conform to the current cultural view of the behavior and what motivates it. If the behavior pattern is seen as problematic, it becomes a symptom of psychopathology with the assumption that some underlying disease or disorder is at play. If the resultant behavior is viewed as conforming to cultural norms, it is either ignored or even encouraged. Some have gone so far as to call it "posttraumatic growth," and they apply the notion that what doesn't kill you makes you stronger (except when it doesn't). More on this later.

This view of psychopathology brings with it the possible iatrogenic impact of clients conforming to expectations of clinicians. When pharmaceutical companies seriously began engaging advertising as a way of promoting psychoactive drug treatments for the various disorders identified in the *DSM*, they matched the benefits of the drug to the language of symptoms as noted in the manual. The proliferation of psychiatric information on the internet also made this type of clinical and professional information available to the general public with little or no explanation, preparation, or guidance. People appeared in our office self-diagnosing themselves with recommendations on drug treatments, likely those having the most advertising rating points in last week's rotation on television. The pattern seemed to go something like this: A given individual hits a rough patch in life and feels out of sorts. They begin complaining to themselves and others of wanting more of something like happiness and contentment and less of whatever is bothering them. The more attention the person gives to the emotions and behaviors that result, the more concerning it becomes. They elicit the opinions of family and friends, and somebody sees a commercial for a new antipsychotic medication used to treat bipolar disorder and notes the symptom of steep mood changes and thinks it fits with themselves or someone they know. They set about researching the diagnosis to see if it fits themselves or the person of interest. They conclude they must have it and seek clinical assistance in overcoming or medicating it.

Example

I (Bill) have received frequent calls from people who have concluded or suspect they have bipolar disorder after a recent television advertising barrage about the drug and what it treats. Occasionally, they may in fact meet the *DSM* criteria for a serious disorder like bipolar disorder, but this often turns out to not be the case. Other possibilities were often explored and based on the results adopted in an effort to move forward. A typical situation entailed a married man—we will call him John—who is in his late 40s who seeks psychotherapy (and perhaps a medication management referral from his primary care physician) for what he thinks is bipolar disorder and reports being moody and irritable, having racing thoughts, and experiencing bursts of energy followed by intense fatigue. He indicates that his spouse of 20 years has been complaining about his moods for several months and that they saw a commercial for a drug that is used to treat bipolar disorder, and after researching it on the internet, he thinks it fits his situation. John reports that these "symptoms" began appearing "out of nowhere" 3 years ago and have been getting worse during the last couple of months. He also reports that his spouse has engaged a couple's counselor to work on their relationship problems. Over the course of the next couple of months, a therapeutic relationship is established with John. He also begins attending couple's counseling where in the fourth couple's session his spouse reveals that she has been having an affair for the past 3 years and wants a divorce. John brings this news to the next session, and he is devastated. "I didn't see this coming at all," he says. As John works through the grief of losing his primary relationship over the course of the next several months, his "symptoms" improve dramatically. John's mood stabilizes, his irritability reduces, racing thoughts become part of his past, and he titrates off the medications his primary care physician prescribed without a relapse of symptoms.

It appears to the therapist and John that having bipolar disorder was preferable to facing the problems that arose over the course of his 20-year marriage. John's "symptoms" might be seen as a coping mechanism that allowed him to make it through each day in a relationship that was not working and served as a way of avoiding the painful truth. On any given day for the prior 3 or so years, his symptoms drew his attention away from his situation to focusing on some underlying psychopathology that a medication and a little therapy would help him manage as opposed to directing his attention to his relationship as a source of the troubles he was experiencing. When we make assumptions about who people are based solely on their complaints, we miss who the person is. We may gain a keen understanding about what they may be experiencing, but little is gained about why this person? Why at this time? What happened? How did it happen? And so on.

The moment you believe that people are more than their history of life events, you begin to see that their symptoms are not indicators of pathology but efforts to right the ship in a storm that continually repeats itself. The fatigue, if viewed differently, is more about the road traveled and not the traveler. If counselors are willing to let go of viewing complaints as problems needing to be solved, then space is provided for clients to not just recover from their history but also be transformed by it.

Witnessing

How do we actually help clients in their various struggles? We have come to understand that empathy is a primary ingredient of effective therapy. How is this achieved? As counselors and psychotherapists, we have received extensive training at identifying, describing, and interpreting a client's experience. We spend a tremendous amount of energy and time educating ourselves to know and understand what makes people "tick." We become experts at identifying what we think of as harmful behavior patterns, signs, and symptoms and then devising interventions to disrupt, disallow, and diminish those patterns, signs, and symptoms. We spend precious little time learning how to get our own experience out of the way of the client's so we can truly join with a given client's experience of their own lives. Our education, assumptions, models, and techniques naturally distance us from our client and safely embed us in our own experience. We often end up with a hodgepodge anecdotal understanding of a person that actually ends up being simply our view of the client through our own eyes and not the client's eyes. We lose touch with the client's experience and shield from it through the filter of our own experience of the problem. Often, all our training and education becomes an impediment to actually joining with our clients where they are in their lives.

This etic view of others is unavoidable in any interaction, as none of us can become the other and live the experience of the other. Yet we can witness the experience of the other as purely as possible. We suggest that the purer the joining, the better the outcomes will be. Witnessing has long been thought to be a part of psychotherapy and counseling, and we as a profession have researched the many various aspects of this process, and at the same time, all this training and knowledge also distances us from our client's experience. Research has demonstrated that the act of witnessing alone has extensive healing potential (Pennebaker, 1988). The act of witnessing creates a container for the client's experience. We often say that just by talking about something it somehow reduces the intensity of the issue being talked about. When we listen intently to the story of another while working to keep our own experience in check, it can have profound impacts on the progress people make in their journey. This activity of listening and witnessing has become known in the field as *processing*. Yet processing is more than just being quiet while another tells their story. Processing experiences has been a part of being human since the dawn of time.

Ancient petroglyphs frequently tell the stories of our ancestors hunting, fighting in battles, gathering, and even being hunted. Modern day graffiti art may be serving the same purpose in many instances. Storytelling has been the treatment of choice for trauma dating back tens of thousands of years. It has been suggested that fairy tales are trauma stories that help create synaptic pathways in the brain or schema that inoculate children to traumas that may happen in the future (Davis, 1996). Organizing storytelling into some sort of therapy ritual happened for a reason. As humans, we all have an amazing capacity to dissociate experience that allows us to pay focused attention on behaviors and strategies that enhance our chances of survival. The fight, flight, and freeze biological responses to fright or being startled are evidence of this fact. Our parasympathetic and sympathetic nervous systems, like many animals, are built around enhancing the odds of survival.

The treatment of trauma has shifted attention to the idea of calming the amygdala (van der Kolk, 2014). We have spent the last 125 years coming up with new and innovative ways to access experience and the dissociated (partial or complete) effect in an effort to calm down the experience associated with efforts to survive or endure trauma and the after-effects. Drama therapy, art therapies, music therapies, primal therapies, somatic therapies, mindfulness therapies, narrative therapies, and more all have as at least one of its desired outcomes processing effects (impacts) in one way or another. Other therapies attempt to reshape affect (emotions): channel it, manage it, stand up to it, shelter from it, build up armor to withstand it, find the meaning in it, affirm it, or express it in one way or another. Being a witness to someone else's story helps reify the experience and facilitate affective expression and processing by creating a container that supports the person telling their story. It is no small wonder that many so-called evidence-based counseling models are structured to formally provide this type of supportive and empathic listening. Prolonged exposure therapy (Foa & Rothbaum, 1998) suggests that this is perhaps one of the most impactful aspects of their brand of accessing and processing traumatic effects. Eye movement and reprocessing therapy (EMDR) is likewise designed in part to access affect and facilitate the brain to bilaterally process the harmful impact associated with traumatic events (Shapiro & Forrest, 1997). It is thought that exposure therapies allow a person to reappraise events and establish meaning and hopefully growth, or what we are calling "posttraumatic growth" (Tedeschi & Calhoun, 1996). These approaches all hinge in part on our capacity to bear witness and our client's capacity to trust us with that experience. They need firm and concrete reasons to place trust in us to be their witnesses. As stated earlier, empathy is an essential ingredient for counseling and psychotherapy to predict positive outcomes (Norcross, 2019; Hubble el al., 2010). We suggest that it is this capacity to be empathic that facilitates the trust that is needed for the witnessing process to be beneficial.

Being a witness to a client's experience is not as easy as it might look. When discussing traumatic events early in the therapy process, clients may speak in a monotone, unaffected, and even emotionless voice. This is evidence that you may be hearing something that has either never been spoken about or not spoken about very much. The affect is often dissociated by the telling and should not be confused with a lack of affect. Other times clients may be quickly overwhelmed and need to retreat from the telling. Our role should be one of accepting and facilitating whatever the client needs to do to secure a position of safety in the unfolding process. In our own anticipation of hearing and witnessing, we may inadvertently push the client past where they are able to contain the devastation they experienced, and this may be retraumatizing for the person and even cause a rupture in the relationship that ends counseling. Some clients may test us with tidbits of a traumatic story to gauge our reactions and tendency to be judgmental. This testing may happen repeatedly early on in the therapeutic relationship and occasionally later on.

Narrative therapy practitioners use a technique they refer to as *outsider witnessing* (Friedman & Combs, 1996). This process is aimed at bringing support from currently or past trusted people (alive or dead) into a client's present to witness the experience of change and healing. They ask questions about what other specific people would say or think about what a client is doing, thinking, feeling, experiencing, and witnessing about the values, their behaviors, goals, and progress the client is engaged in as they progress through the therapy process. This outsider witnessing is thought to add credibility and reification to self-identified positive steps the client is taking, or contemplating based on values and actions the client has identified as preferred having as a part of their identity. This type of process allows the client to get third-party affirmation and expands the experience of positive reinforcement surrounding new insights, ideas, changes, and attitudes. It also supports the meaning-making process and situates the client in a milieu of shared experience as opposed to one of isolation.

In 1983, Wheeler and his team created an experiment that concluded that a single photon beam can be either a wave or particle. The implications of their research and quantum mechanics were that a photon does not have definite or intrinsic properties until observed, that in the space between the beginning and the end is something undecided, awaiting to be seen so that both shape and direction can be determined. As people are constantly in the state of becoming, so too are their resilient qualities awaiting to be seen. A photon becomes a particle or wave depending on how the beam interacts with its surroundings. People can be seen as victims of their histories and the stories of defeat in response to overwhelming adversity and emotion or seen as remarkable given all they have to confront. The space in between is the space that provides clients a choice, the possibility to act more like a wave with the ability to adapt, change, and evolve rather than a particle that moves only in a straight line. Particle-oriented counselors ask too many questions, directly or indirectly give advice to others, and, with good intent, reassure.

All questions are biased, giving light to the stance and intent of the questioner. If focused on understanding story details rather than on a shared understanding of the storyteller's experience of the story as they tell it, the only pathway available for the counselor and client is problem solving. It highlights a stance where the desires of the counselor for the client take precedence over what the client wishes for themselves. As one supervisee once quoted to me, "If I could just ask the right question, they would see what I see for them." When the counselor is preoccupied with putting the pieces of the story together, it leads to an overuse of closed-ended questions and content summaries; and when clinical listening becomes content heavy on facts, events, and consequences, the only available interventions are problem-solving strategies. Although these strategies may have potential benefit, if offered prematurely, this teaching intervention can result in clients defending the status quo in response to a counselor's benevolent suggestions for personal change. It is a stance of privilege and quickly diminishes the client's agency in the eyes of both counselor and client. If a counselor believes in the inherent resources available to people when shoring up against life's struggles, then a wondrous curiosity to their experience, seeking to "lead from behind," provides the acknowledgment needed to make the previously unknown qualities of resilience acknowledged.

Example

In my experience as a counseling supervisor, I (Colin) will often hear a counselor complain that their therapeutic conversations with a particular client are becoming circular and repetitious. "It's as if," they will say, "we are having the same conversation in different ways." They will, with some resignation, express that "there must be more to their story." McGilchrist (2009) referred to this as a *left hemisphere loop*. The left hemisphere of the brain, adept at organizing stored experiences, seeks solutions to avoid discrepancies. When memories of the past are not sufficient to make an orderly and logical understanding of a disorienting experience, the right hemisphere is called upon to provide more creative ways of knowing. Chronic stress or trauma can interfere with how the two hemispheres communicate via the corpus callosum, leaving individuals in a constant state of worry and rumination. The counselor's need to find answers parallels the same obsession the client has for reassurance. And so the loop continues, each wishing to find the missing piece of the puzzle and, in so doing, finding only the client's familiar feeling of helplessness.

As noted previously, if the goal of counseling is to assist others in withstanding and soothing themselves in the face of overwhelming stress and life events, then to do this for them is to imply that they cannot do this for themselves. Assisting clients to work from the bottom up with somatic and affect regulation is not only best practice but also illuminates the power of mind-body medicine. By noting the experience of the story rather than the story itself, opportunities for clients to self-soothe will emerge. In fact, the space in between is the space that invites imagination, multiple ways of seeing the world, and a broader sense of who people are and wish to become. Acceptance and gratitude reside in the right hemisphere and, when acknowledged, has been demonstrated to reduce worry and increase self-narratives of efficacy or competence (Davidson, 2012).

Top Takeaways

1. Individuals experiencing learned helplessness often just appear to do the same thing over and over and choose to remain in adverse and even torturous circumstances long after escape becomes possible and even encouraged.

2. Once again, the tendency is to blame the person for the behavior without a clear contextual understanding of the demand characteristics present in an individual's local and larger culture. Feminist psychologists took issue with this approach to diagnosing and pathologizing people for engaging in behaviors that enhanced their survival and successfully fought to keep this diagnosis out of *DSM-IV* in 1994.

3. It has been suggested over the years that traumatic reenactments are simply failed attempts to have a "do over" in an effort to make the outcome different. This may in fact be the case and an area in need of attention by counselors.

4. If counselors are willing to let go of viewing complaints as problems needing to be solved, then space is provided for clients to not just recover from their history but to be transformed by it.

5. Narrative counseling allows the client to get third-party affirmation and expands the experience of positive reinforcement surrounding new insights, ideas, changes, and attitudes. It also supports the meaning-making process and situates the client in a milieu of shared experience as opposed to one of isolation.

Postmodernism

Postmodernism contends that human experiences (and one's perception of it) are far too complex to be described in two dimensional terms ... It is an acceptance of the unique, meaningful experiences of others and the inherent wisdom and strengths they bring to the change process.

—Ward & Reuter (2011, p.13)

The postmodern evolution in psychotherapy did not just suddenly appear out of the blue. There were glimmerings of it throughout the 20th century from many different corners: Adler's emphasis on society as a formative factor in personality in the early part of the 1900s, Carl Rogers's focus on the client process and belief that people want to change in positive ways and do not knowingly set out to engage in maladaptive behavior, Viktor Frankl's assertion that life is about the meaning we derive from it and that suffering begets resilience, and Milton Erickson's stance that people have all the resources they need to live fulfilled lives. The feminist critique broadened focus to multicultural issues and social justice as well as working to create more egalitarian collaborative therapeutic relationships in order to achieve therapeutic goals of empowerment, efficacy, and activism. Ideas about simultaneously considering multiple perspectives on a client's lived experience absent of labels that may be oppressive and laden with cultural stigma were emerging. Situating the "problem" in the larger sociocultural context as well as the client's structural system(s) became an easy and natural next step in the evolutionary process of a psychotherapy informed by family system theories. These overlapping ideas of the human experience, developed over the past several decades, emphasized a constructed nature of knowledge where the world, and our experience of it, exist in the eyes and mind unique to each beholder. As such, a collaborative approach utilizing client assets and setting aside diagnosis in favor of presenting "complaints" was emphasized.

In general, postmodern approaches do not posit real truths about the human experience. Comb's (1954) early theory on perception explained "how a person behaves will be a direct outgrowth of the perceptions existing at any moment" (p. 65). These perceptions are constantly in a state of revision influenced by interaction with others, culture, and society at large. In other words, it is not so much an understanding of multiple realities as it is that our perception of ourselves and the world around us is unique, varied, and constantly being added to or revised. This perception is understood as a self-narrative: an internal conversation of who we are in relation to our surroundings at any given moment in time. It is how our beliefs about ourselves and our surroundings are developed. In many respects, it is this belief structure that constitutes our perception of reality. As Jones-Smith (2019) noted, "It is not until individuals change their belief system that they can change their reality and their performance" (p. 135). Postmodern approaches address oppressing self-narratives that diminish one's worth through a mutual consideration of other possible life stories that might also be true. These invitations are designed to thicken or enrich the beliefs of oneself with elements of agency and efficacy (e.g., "I'm wondering if your fatigue might also reflect the weight of responsibility you carry for others?"). Assisting others to absorb, integrate, and make use of multiple perspectives can assist with affect regulation and tolerating ambiguity when life choices all have both benefits and pitfalls. This, in turn, creates more openness to varied experiences, awareness of individual differences, and a critical consciousness that can consider oppression in their own lives as well as hold a sensitivity to the oppression in the lives of others (Granello, 2010; Lawrence et al., 2015; Vera & Spreight, 2003).

A postmodern-oriented counselor considers life and people far more complex than what is implied by a binary worldview of change. Wellness is more than the absence of disease. Meaningful self-discovery and relationships cannot be fully achieved by merely replacing an unwanted thought or behavior. Consider the Grand Canyon. I (Colin) have hiked this location a half a dozen times, from the heat of summer to the freeze of winter. I have viewed each ridge in the morning sunlight and acknowledged the final rays of the day as the sun set below the horizon. Even though this wonderous geological formation has changed little in the past millennia, it looked different each time, depending on where and when I experienced it. The intent of postmodern counseling is to assist others with viewing and describing their world from multiple and broader points of view. This becomes an appreciation of the canyon and the light reflected upon it, the hiker, and the relationship between all three (i.e., the canyon, the light, and the hiker). By highlighting the struggle of another not from a deficit perspective but from a place of appreciation where all perspectives are layered in truth, client self-narratives are broadened and revised to include a wider range of options for self-determined change—in essence, a recovery of choices. In many ways, as we review the features and approaches of postmodernism, counselors join their clients as they consider the varying views, and the meaning therein, to the vast canyons of their lived experiences.

Multiplicity

Through a lens of multiplicity, clients are viewed as experts on who they are and are becoming. The counselor promotes a relationship that is, as much as possible, nonjudgmental and accepting of the client's experiences, world views, and the inherent resilient qualities they present in the face of life's challenges. As Lambert (1992) pointed out in his review of counseling outcomes, the counseling relationship can empower and motivate people in the process of change. As an empathic participant in the counseling process, the counselor becomes a "curious conversationalist" (Miller, 2001, p. 80). This unique kind of listening requires counselors to acquire an ever-expanding curious tolerance for diverse views and has been associated with such traits as openness, appreciation of difference, multicultural competence, ambiguity tolerance, and an awareness to the multifaceted nature of people and how problems are often outcomes associated with social and cultural influences (Lawrence et al., 2015). It is a holistic way of thinking that is inviting and inclusive. It is "both/and" rather than "either/or" where all experiences and perspectives are unique and important. Even more critically, however, to hold a stance of multiplicity is to be imminently focused on the other's understanding of themselves and their place in the world. It is a stance of utter nonjudgment and reflects a shared understanding of the struggles, values, and suffering inferred in the problem-saturated narratives that clients often express. This shared understanding does not mean that the counselor must hold the same viewpoint or experience; rather, it requires the counselor to listen not simply to client's problems and the stories surrounding them but to look more deeply at who clients are, within their own unique context, and, more importantly, who they wish to be. So often therapists become preoccupied with understanding what clients wish to *do*, they neglect the essential question of who they wish to *become*: what values they hold, what or who they wish to be in service to, how they hope to evolve and adapt in the face of life struggles, the relationships they hope to mend, and the wisdom and strengths they may desire to hold closer. For the clinician, developing a tolerance to respect varying opinions and life experiences vastly different from their own requires a commitment of the counselor to also turn this same intent inward, to hold the mirror and consider:

- Can I accept the varied and dissonant experiences of another's experience if I have not done so myself?
- What are the stories of my own resilient efforts and the strengths I have tapped into in order to keep one foot in front of the other?
- How do I experience myself with regard to my gender, race, sexual orientation, culture, and socioeconomic status? In what ways might this limit or hinder my ability to hold dissimilar identities?

You find in others what you believe to be true in yourself. If you have faith in the unique and surprising resources of people as they confront the often-insurmountable odds to a better life, you will find such. If you hold yourself with compassion, understanding, and a tenacious belief in your own resilient nature, you open space for others to do the same. It is through these shared connections of respect that a mutual faith develops: a faith in the possible, regardless of the risks, and a faith in one another. This is resilient counseling: a humble undertaking that there but by the grace of God go I.

Activity: Inherent Wisdoms

This text promotes a liberating approach that invites people to take their power back from whatever trauma, biological fact, differently abled condition, or oppression they are experiencing or have been exposed to.

1. In dyads, have a shared conversation about the wisdom you hope to take from a current struggle or life event.
2. What do these wisdoms say about your deepest values? Which of these would you like to hold closer during the upcoming week?

REMINDER: As a listener, refrain from benevolent statements of privilege (e.g., "That's great" or "Good for you"). Engage with checkouts of understanding only.

Take a moment to look around. Take your attention to the distance as well as those objects much closer. You will begin to feel strain on your eyes as they seek a coordinated movement so that a single point on your retina is maintained. As you look at a nearby object, your eyes move inward and converge so that you might better read this page or work your phone. Similarly, when gazing at the horizon, your eyes diverge outward so the depth and breadth of your perspective increases.

From a multiplicity perspective, resiliency can best be understood not as a fixed idea or set of actions but as a divergent landscape of concepts and dimensions harnessed by clinicians to enhance the resilient qualities of themselves and their clients. A convergence that looks inward sees the inherent worth of the self and others, often in ways unimaginable to either the counselor or client. A convergence accentuating a trust in the wisdom and strength obtained through the strain of adversity, where clients, not counselors, are the experts on their own experiences emerges. These attributes can serve as a light when stumbling around in the dark. This convergence reveals the undeniable truth that resilient living cannot occur in isolation but in connection with others: a striving to be of service to one's personal integrity as well as to one's culture, family, and community. In much the same way that our eyes adjust as we look around, so too does activating our natural inclination toward renewal and self-healing. As we focus inward on our strengths, values, and personal qualities, space is opened to see how these insights might be applied as our gaze looks out to the horizon. It has little to do with solving problems, prescribing treatment, or seeking to benevolently heal another and more to do with counselors holding space so that people may discover for themselves the strength, wisdom, and understanding needed to open and gain a vantage over the oppressive impact of trauma and adversity so that they may be in greater service to their deepest ideals as well as to the communities in which they live.

Bugenthal (1987) contended that counselors "need only to begin ... [and to] ... enter the encounter without concern about its exact nature or outcome" (p. 90). This then is the starting point for multiplicity, whereby seeking to hold space without forming an agenda, clients are more apt to share their unique experiences and perspectives without fear of judgment. In these experiences, it is important that the psychotherapist consider the various layers of the client's context, their immediate relationships and their situated identity within their local and larger communities and structural systems.

Example

On a Friday when I was working as a counselor at a local college, I (Katherine) was wrapping up a day of back-to-back clients and preparing to teach a weekend course on stress management. Ironically, I was feeling stressed to get things done quickly in order to head over to my classroom across campus when I got a call from our intake desk. A student, Anna, had arrived late in the afternoon and was asking to connect with me, a counselor that she knew in passing. The counseling center had an open-door policy, so the front desk rang my office to see if I could talk with her. Instead of powering down my computer, I sat back down to invite her in. In the first 5 minutes, I struggled to be present; my mind was already in the start of class. But in slowing down my own breath, her story emerged. At first, she shared concern about her uncle's anger management and let me know that she lived with her grandparents. I began to form an agenda to work with her on a safety plan to stay away from her uncle and to tell the rest of her family about her fear of his

(Continued)

outbursts when she shared the further complexity of the story. As it turned out, Anna's biological mother was permanently hospitalized due to mental illness, her grandfather was ill, and neither of her grandparents spoke English and relied on her for communication support. Her grandmother was physically and emotionally abusive toward her and her uncle, the family breadwinner, was the one in control of the home, a place where she was unsafe and did not want to return.

In my initial conversation, I had assumed numerous cultural and contextual attributes that were not true for this first-generation Vietnamese American woman. On the outside, she appeared to be entirely in control of her life: She had straight As, came to school put together, and had a gregarious and friendly affect. But as we talked and as I slowed down and really listened, I let go of my assumptions one by one. I began to slow down and really listen. As a result, she felt enough trust in our relationship to tell me more and more of the contextual challenges in her situation. Her grandparents were her guardians but did not work, her uncle paid for her schooling, and in return, she was expected to keep quiet about the abuse in the home; the deeply traumatic physical and emotional abuse toward her by both him and her grandmother each day. This abuse and the manual labor that she was expected to perform—cooking and cleaning for everyone in order to "earn her keep"—was so awful, she feared for her life.

We spent that afternoon calling local shelters to try and find her a safe space for the night, and she decided that she would emancipate herself from the situation and never go back. Ultimately, we were able to connect with a previous teacher in her life who took her in and later would informally "adopt" her. Had I not slowed down, deeply listened, and set aside my assumptions, the trust needed for her to share more about the depth of her challenges and safety issues would not have been there. Had I kept my agenda to move through our work in a quick 50 minutes, she would not have had someone seated by her side, making calls to help her find safety. In the end, Anna went on to graduate with her bachelor's degree, and when she graduated, she reminded me of the power of that day, when we sat in community. Although I was quick to tell her that it was her own strength that had moved her out and through such adversity, she described that day as the day that we sat together and saved her life.

Meaningful Dialogues

Santamaria (1990) contended that people do not belong to the world; they exist in a world of possibilities that become realities through their conscious interpretation. In this, it is less about the stories of suffering shared with counselors and more about how stories define the storyteller: an attunement to the *experience* of what is being said. This requires counselors to accept, without reservation, the worldview of clients, appreciate what they wish to be different, and remain curious about how our stories can both maintain despair as well as remind them of their strengths and introduce hope and possibilities. Therapeutic change occurs through experiencing a constructed truth within the client–counselor interaction rather than an absolute truth discovered solely by the therapist. This constructed truth between the client and counselor is largely an experience of meaning. It is through stories, woven within experience, that people make sense of their lives and themselves. In conversation and interaction with others, life stories are ascribed meanings that are used to define one's sense of self, shape behavior, and orient oneself in the world (Dimaggio et al., 2003; Hansen, 2007; Hoffman et al., 2009; Maturana & Varela, 1987).

Since the constructed truth between the client and counselor is largely an experience of language, the strategic use of language to elicit new meanings, expand perspectives, and encourage change is central to a postmodern approach of counseling. This language assists helping professionals shift from seeing only risk to seeing resilience and strength while highlighting people's choices. It also creates an assumption of accountability rather than blame or determinism. As Bertolino and O'Hanlon (2002) articulated, "If the person is not the problem, but has a certain relationship to the problem, then the relationship can change. … If the problem is trying to recruit a client, he or she can refuse to join" (p. 133). When taking a stance of multiplicity, counselors open space for clients to do the same. It is a reflective process that provides a pause, a noticing, and a consideration of additional perspectives and understandings that may also be true. A former client once referred to this as "stepping back from the chalkboard" to consider, with as little self-judgment or criticism as possible, alternative ways of seeing the same thing … together.

This reflective dynamic is a central aspect of trauma recovery toward developing a felt sense of safety and relaxation when integrating dissociated and suppressed trauma experiences (Gentry et al., 2015). It is described as the process whereby people meaningfully reconstruct experiences utilizing a repertoire of understandings, images, and actions to reconstruct a troubling situation so that problem-solving interventions can be generated (Ward & House, 1998). Reflective counselors examine their beliefs and assumptions in response to *dissonant clinical experiences* so as to deepen their understanding of the client, of themselves, and of their relationship together. In contrast to modernist or traditional approaches of counseling that can seek to reduce client discomfort, a postmodern gaze utilizes discomfort to guide counselors in their practice and assist clients in marshalling resilience. Reflectivity is an openness in the face of disequilibrium.

The anterior cingulate cortex (ACC) is in a unique position in that it lies between the "emotional" limbic region of the brain and the "cognitive" prefrontal cortex. It is partly responsible for how reality is filtered and assists with processing whether we are safe or threatened. When stress hormones are released, the ACC diminishes in function and "individuals will stop making decisions based on sensory information and begin to make decisions based on previous experiences. … This can result in a perceived threat where in reality there is none" (Dubi et al., 2017, p. 17). In essence, the electrical activity needed to engage executive functions for rational responses are reduced, and protective reactions ensue. It is not so much the dissonance of experience that diminishes our ability for reflective meaning making but our tolerance for dissonance in the experiences themselves. Haase (2016) contended that since the ACC is surrounded by the limbic system and the cortical executive regions, this may explain why somatic awareness, or mindfulness, reduces impulsivity and increases emotional regulation. This is the choice to pause, to slow one's breath, and to notice ourselves, as if stepping back from the chalkboard. This is similar to Meichenbaum's (1985) inoculation training that espoused that exposure to stress, with increased confidence management, increases resilience. To hold our experience of stress while still having access to higher order thinking increases an individual's ability to respond with flexibility.

In fact, the intentional awareness of internal sensations can lead to enhanced self-regulation and access to positive internal resources. Reflecting on our strengths is both calming and empowering. This is true for both the counselor and the client and is especially critical in their work together. This early approach to trauma-informed therapy entails engaging in the cognitive and executive functions of the brain while invoking imaginary traumatic events that simultaneously activate protective responses. Eye movement desensitization and reprocessing therapy (EMDR) mirrors this approach by engaging the client in concentrating on following a moving light or hand with their eyes, or listening to sound moving from one ear to the other, or alternating tapping on one side of the body and the other while recalling actual traumatic events, which creates this double attention, allowing executive function to remain online while activating the protective affective responses in a more controlled fashion (Shapiro, 1997).

Frank (1987) asserted that therapeutic interaction is successful only to the extent that it helps clients transform the meaning of their experiences. If counselors can hold the dissonance associated with viewing others from varying and often competing perspectives while assisting others in doing the same, then space for personal meaning is available. To catch oneself and look inward, to refrain from merely reacting from protective defenses, and to respond with openness to the possible and that many things can be true from a single experience means that resilience has a chance, not just in that moment but in the moments to follow.

Approaches

So how would you approach clients differently if your assumption is that clients are the experts on their own lives and have all the resources needed for the change they desire? What might you listen for with others that you are not hearing now? What inquiries might you make and questions would you seek to answer? If you fully believed in the inherent strength and restorative dynamics of people, how might you prepare for each session differently? What might you stop doing? These are the questions that Steve De Shazer, Insoo Berg, and Eve Lipchik sought to address as they developed a solution-focused approach to counseling as well as Michael White and David Epston in their development of narrative therapy. As noted by Bertolino and O'Hanlon (2002), postmodernism required clinicians to shift from conversations of explanation, inability, insight, and transference into intentional conversations with clients focused on change, competence, possibilities, and action. These change-oriented questions represent a significant shift in therapeutic intent from widely used modern paradigms of counseling (e.g., consciousness and empiricism) to those consistent with a more postmodern paradigm (see Table 7.1).

TABLE 7.1 Comparing Modern and Postmodern Paradigms

Modern paradigm	Postmodern paradigm
• Personality theories (unprovable)	• Life is difficult (people as resilient)
• Empiricism (people as puzzles)	• Life is meaningful (meaningful dialogues)
• Past and pathology (emphasis on deficits)	• Present and future (emphasis on strengths)
• Singular truth (to be discovered)	• Multiple truths (multiplicity and co-construction)
• Singular experience (binary and sequential)	• Multiple experiences (simultaneous both/and)
• Problems to be solved (first order)	• Solutions to be constructed (second order)
• Counselor as healer (prescriptive)	• Client as healer (collaborative)

At its core solution-focused therapy (SFT) is collaborative, assuming that people and families had both the resources and capacity for change. As Eve Lipchik (2011) noted, "Therapists don't change clients, clients change themselves" (p. 7). She also cautioned against well-meaning counselors seeking to relieve clients of their pain, becoming too protective from their suffering rather than helping them use their own resources, strengths, and capabilities to take care of themselves. As De Jong and Berg (1998) noted:

> Wittingly or unwittingly, the helping professions have encouraged practitioners to believe and act as though their perceptions about their clients' problems and solutions are more important to the helping process than are the clients' perceptions. (p. 19)

This highlights the simple truth that living is hard. The very act of surviving life's hardships and withstanding the toll of chronic stress and then finding a way to show up in our offices and agencies is a testament to client's inherent strength and the resilient nature of the human spirit. Similarly, narrative therapy (NT) is grounded in the existential idea that individuals are unique in how they relate to the experiences of their lives (Kierkegaard, 1954) as well as to the internal perception they have of themselves. If these internal perceptions become problem saturated, self-denigrating beliefs and emotional suffering can result. The intent of NT is to assist individuals and families with eliciting new aspects of their stories so that unique outcomes can be constructed as well as future perceptions of themselves and others (White, 1989). Whereas solution-focused counselors invite clients and families to construct a conceptual model of their futures with concrete evidence as to how their growth will be recognized (Cepeda & Davenport, 2006), the intent of narrative counselors is to assist individuals and families with eliciting new aspects of their stories so that unique outcomes can be constructed as well as future perceptions of themselves and others (White, 1989). Furthermore, individuals often enter counseling enmeshing their sense of self with their problems.

Both SFT and NT utilize prompts or open questions to shift the dialogue between counselor and client in very intentional ways consistent with a postmodern paradigm and the specific focus of each approach. Table 7.2 compares the use of questions in this very intentional way. They are not interventions or techniques but invitations for collaborative conversations of change, competence, and choice. Consider a current problem pattern in your own life and write your initial responded to the questions below. Notice your experience as well as how the story of yourself in relationship to your problem pattern shifts, even just a little bit. Opening space for a slightly different of view ourselves is the essence of a postmodern perspective. How might you continue to do this with yourself and invite others to do the same?

TABLE 7.2 Invitations for Collaborative Change

Solution-focused therapy (exceptions)	Narrative counseling (opening space)
• What is different about you when you are more able to keep your head above water? What is your guess on how you are able to do that at those times?	• What does the problem wish you to believe about yourself? What has influenced this belief (e.g., family, culture, socio/political climate)?
• What is different about those times when things are a bit more on track for you? What is your guess about how you are able to keep the problem at bay a bit better?	• What have these ideas of yourself robbed you of?
	• How much of your life does it control? Are you ok with this? What is it like to say out loud?
• When the problem is less present, what are you thinking about instead? What ideas and activities seem more available?	• Do you think it is best for {problem} to run your life, or would it be better to run your own life?
• What is your guess about what others might notice in you when the problem is less present?	• What do you imagine might be different about you if you took back even a small bit of your life?

Top Takeaways

1. Postmodernism contends that it is not so much an understanding of "multiple realities" as it is that our perception of ourselves and the world around us is unique, varied, and constantly being added to or revised.

2. A postmodern-oriented counselor considers life and people as far more complex than what is implied by a binary worldview of change. Wellness is more than the absence of disease, and meaningful self-discovery and relationships cannot be fully achieved by merely replacing an unwanted thought or behavior.

3. Resilience from a postmodern perspective has little to do with solving problems, prescribing treatment, or seeking to benevolently heal another and more to do with counselors holding space so that people may discover for themselves the strength, wisdom, and understanding needed to gain vantage over the oppressive impact of trauma and adversity so that they may be in greater service to their deepest ideals as well as to the communities in which they live.

4. At its core solution-focused therapy (SFT) is collaborative, assuming that people and families have both the resources and capacity for change.

5. The intent of NC is to assist individuals and families with eliciting new aspects of their stories so that unique outcomes can be constructed as well as future perceptions of themselves and others.

Feminism and Resilience

The struggle is inner: Chicano, indio, American Indian, mojado, mexicano, immigrant Latino, Anglo in power, working class Anglo, Black, Asian—our psyches resemble the border towns and are populated by the same people. The struggle has always been inner, and is played out in outer terrains. Awareness of our situation must come before inner changes, which in turn come before changes in society. Nothing happens in the "real" world unless it first happens in the images in our heads.

—Gloria Anzaldúa (1987, p. 87)

A Brief History

Historically, psychology and counseling theories have been based in Western, male-centric, individualistic ideology. The goal of most of these theories was to "fix" the individual, and as a consequence, sociosystem-related issues were ignored (if they were even seen in the first place). As the women's liberation movement took hold in the United States during the 1960s, so too did a shift in the psychological assessment of women and how best to support women emotionally through a feminist, intellectually aligned ideology. It was the impetus for the founding of many new structures of mental health care for women in the 1970s and 1980s (Crook, 2018). Pat Mainardi, a member of the New York Redstockings collective (a consciousness-raising group during the women's liberation movement), wrote a piece entitled "The Politics of Housework" in 1970. Her writing was humorous yet critically outlined the ways that the assumptions and related tasks of housework had served as an oppressive force against women for centuries. Written work, such as Mainardi's, was profoundly influential in opening the eyes of women to themselves, their potential for greater societal value, their desire to be seen, and also to the flawed systems of which they were a part. As the movement took hold across most industrialized Western countries, "women's issues," which had once been upheld as individual flaws in meeting women's expected gender roles, were turned over, revealing oppressive systems where women could not possibly meet their full potential as human beings. This revelation had a massive impact on the field of counseling, where postmodern approaches to psychotherapy and social constructivist theory were more heavily adopted and the value of "co-construction" of meaning gained deeper traction. Feminism, in turn, impacted those theories further by highlighting the fact that the person is not always the problem; oftentimes, the person is the resilient survivor of a problematic and oppressive system.

The Privileged Clinician

A common perception of clinicians, even a subconscious one, is that individuals coming to therapy share a common set of privileged assets. More specifically, clients who are able to utilize the support of a therapist who works in private practice must, to a certain degree, have the capacity (agency) to do so via a multitude of logistical assets: economic, physical, and linguistic, to name a few. Clients must understand how to research and find a counselor, usually navigating countless websites and referral sources. They must have the capacity to go online and read, to make phone calls in English, and to set aside any self-doubt or sense of shame that may be percolating in their mind. They may have to combat their internal narrative and conceptualization of those who seek help as weak or sick, pushing down shame and stigma. Community mental health may reduce some of these barriers, but this system also raises other hurdles: more limited availability, a complex and inefficient system, and counselor burnout. In both cases, clients arrive at counseling after intentional action and likely some difficulty in seeking and obtaining support.

The lens through which counselors see their clients is often based on assumptions of agency and individualism. In essence, clients are conceptualized through a predominantly White, European/European American/Western ideology. Even when we work to push back on those assumptions, these views are still housed within our subconscious, situated in our minds based on our own socio-cultural experiences and received messages from the field and in our educational history. We wrongly assume that it is our job to "empower" our clients—as though it is a gift that we hold and one that we can choose to bestow. As you have read in the preceding chapters, the related fields of counseling and psychology have grown to embrace a social constructivist and postmodern lens, yet still these professions must operate in step with the medical model in order to receive both funding and validation. While arguably effective, many of the evidence-based approaches utilized by community mental health and medical professions and taught in counselor education programs are rooted in a worldview that predates the more current drive for holism, cultural competence, and social justice.

The Trouble with "Empowerment"

Not all counseling professionals take the time to humbly self-reflect on the power or privilege that they bring to the counseling space. Many counselors have held these positions of power and have purposefully and willingly looked away from the race, gender, or intersectional elements of their student, patient, or client in an attempt to be *less* sexist or racist. Many fear that looking straight on at their systemic advantage may further distance themselves from their clients or that they may say the wrong thing and cause harm, so it is better to be quiet, better to be "blind." Except, in the end, none of us is actually blind to oppression. We know it like the back of our hand. As stated earlier, it has been passed down to us, generation to generation. In much the same way that dissonance stimulates the restorative capacity for change and renewal, the sooner mental health professionals look at and face up to these oppressive forces—albeit uncomfortable—the more we can actually create systemic change. What happens to the client when their counselor, so often the more privileged person in the room (due to educational access and inherent power structures present within the relationship itself), intentionally looks away from such foundational and impactful aspects of identity? Do we empower others in our effort to look away, or is resilience-centered counseling about providing a space where clients find their power? We argue, of course, the latter. It is our job to recognize not only the various contextual identities in the counselor/client dynamic but also the intersectionality present in the room, the elements of the client's identity as well as our own, and, finally, how all of these interact to form the unique capacity of this relationship of healing and mutual growth. To say that we do not also grow in this work would be to continue to hold on to a harmful professional narrative of the past.

Unpacking Assumption

Looking back on how early psychoanalytic approaches approached female clients, we can see that clinicians were guided by their socio-cultural conceptualizations of female cultural roles of mother, wife, and daughter. Women's expression of therapeutic concerns in the clinical setting were often categorized in demeaning and declassifying behaviors, linked to excessive emotionality, hormonal "imbalances," or flights of fancy beyond reality. The gaze that clinicians brought to the counseling relationship thus influenced not only how counselors perceived clients but also, more importantly, how clients viewed themselves. Instead of focusing on internal strengths and resilience, female clients were encouraged to work on "letting go," "moving on," and reducing expectations.

In the training process, counselors are often taught to view "theory" as a set of assumptions on which to rest their "understandings about human behavior, the essence of mental health and illness, and the various factors to which an individual's status may be attributed" (Ballou et al., 2008, p. 67). Essentially, theory informs the way that we not only think about our client's presenting problem but also how we view our clients in contextual terms. As humans, it is our nature to subconsciously assess and classify one another into categories (e.g., biological sex, gender expression, race, size, and level of fitness, to name the most common classifiers in today's era). For counselors, assumptions and value judgements can reactively occur beyond their immediate awareness. Unless an effort is made to deconstruct these reactive biases, rooted in membership to a privileged class, counselors will not be able to open the space necessary for others to apply their own voice of agency and influence in their lives.

Interrupting Categorical Thinking and Implicit Bias

Philosopher Jacques Derrida described Western thought as structured in terms of dichotomies or polarities (good vs. evil, being vs. nothingness, presence vs. absence, truth vs. error, identity vs. difference, mind vs. matter, man vs. woman, etc.). He continued to say that these opposites do not stand as equal but that the second term in each pair is considered the undesirable version of the first arranged in a hierarchical order which gives them "first priority" (Derrida, 1981, vii). Such culturally laden categorical thinking exaggerates the worth of one at the expense of the other. When we uphold one identity as "good" or "strong," we see the perceived converse of that identity as "bad" or "weak." Western thought has created little space for the multitude of identities and experiences between the perceived poles. When we expect people to fit squarely in the bookends, we practice oppressive assumptions and expectations consistent with the structures of sexism and racism. To marginalize one group in favor of another is to fracture, separate, and divide. It is to devalue another's autonomy. When clinicians are unaware of this bias, they practice in arrogance and judgment, ultimately robbing others of dignity, respect, and resources. The very thing needed for change to occur is the very thing diminished in the process of helping.

It is the tireless work of social justice advocacy that asks us to work to identify and untether those internal biases that all humans inherently hold. We know the importance of this when we reflect on how the worst of these biases have caused mass genocide and dehumanization on historical and global scales for thousands of years. Bonhoeffer (1940) believed that the unchecked judging of one's peers has the capacity to deteriorate a whole society. We have seen this history repeat itself through colonization, political extremism, and religious persecution. Today, we see the harmful impacts of this polarization in the American sociopolitical landscape. As a primary characteristic of abuse, marginalizing groups infer certain identities as "worthless" or a "threat to the fundamental values and beliefs of the assignees" (Dubois et al., 2012). Marginalization creates feelings of helplessness, isolation, and a general loss of self.

As discussed earlier, for many years counselors have been taught to conceptualize their clients through a presenting problem. This problem was often unpacked through categorical thinking about who our client is via their roles and/or "place" in society. For example, mothers may be diagnosed with postpartum depression, yet not much focus is given to men who may feel similar anxieties and/or sadness regarding the changes or challenges that so often come with raising a child. According to the Centers for Disease Control and Prevention (2021), boys are 3 times more likely to receive an ADHD diagnosis than girls, yet not much research has been focused on young women who may feel similar challenges maintaining focus on their schoolwork. This is not to say that these struggles are not real, critical to our society, or justifiably consuming for the client. The point here is to slow down our assumptions when we think about mental health issues in relation to gender. In Western society and in our field, we still look at a woman's adaptation to the role of being a mother and for men the importance of scholastic achievement and, in turn, career advancement.

Reflecting on how these social norms and assumptions impact clients, Gilligan and her colleagues found that girls silence themselves related to their desires, abilities, and interests on the belief that this may lead to more intimate relationships (Gilligan, 1982; Taylor et al., 1995). Consistent with other findings, the higher the perception of masculinity, the greater perceived mental health. Over history, the impact of this discrimination has led to a greater prevalence of mood and eating disorders in women as well borderline, dependent, and histrionic disorders (Nehls, 1998). This is especially apparent in those that identify as nonbinary. In a recent study, Lefevor et al. (2019) found that genderqueer individuals experience more anxiety, depression, and psychological distress than cisgender individuals. This is consistent with minority stress, where prejudice events, stigma, and discrimination create a hostile and stressful environment resulting in mental health distress and related problems (Meyer, 2003). These experiences bear out in statistics on suicide ideation and attempts by those who identify as LGBTQ, showing that they are 4 times as likely to attempt suicide than non-LGBTQ youth (The Trevor Project, 2021). As human beings, when we are told that our value is less than others in society, we tend to internalize those feelings as truth.

Resilience occurs via connection to both ourselves and others. It is not that marginalized groups are less resilient; it is that the very nature of their lived experiences reduces access to the conditions where resilience can grow and thrive. This repression is repeated in compounding ways that not only reduce access but also, most problematically, reduce hope for anything different. By experiencing a nonjudgmental, accepting, and respectful therapeutic relationship, clients are introduced to a context where hope can occur, and human connection can be both experienced and nurtured.

The Impact of Oppression Is Exponential

Race is a social construct, invented to categorically place various melanin levels of skin tone at either advantage (lighter skin tones) or disadvantage (darker skin tones) in relation to systems of economic prosperity. Human beings have been forcibly and abusively pushing other human beings into laboring for free or reduced wages for hundreds, if not thousands, of years. These experiences and expectations of normality within such inhumane treatment have also passed through the ages in the form of generational family and societal trauma, described in Resmaa Menakem's (2017) book *My Grandmothers Hands*. His work teaches us, both the counselor and the client, that we carry this historical trauma in our lived bodily experience every day, no matter our racial identity. We are all affected by the larger systems of oppression in the world, and the first step toward healing—both personally and as a community—is in developing an awareness of these impacts.

Similar to societal assumptions made along the gender line by those in positions of power within our field, helping professionals have historically turned a blind eye to the impact of race on both the individual experience of the client and on the racial dynamics present within the counseling relationship. Even when racial justice began to enter the space of clinical perception, largely in the 1980s, assimilation and "color blindness" became the ideal racial enlightenment thinking, further ignoring the BIPOC (black, indigenous, and people of color) experience. Today, much of the United States' culture and, more importantly, governing systems describe racism as the "outright formal exclusion of people of color," thus deeming American culture, schools, workplaces, and neighborhoods "racially and culturally neutral" so long as they do not categorically and formally exclude specific racial groups from public services (Crenshaw et al., 1995).

> *Today, blacks experiencing rejection for a job, a home, a promotion anguish over whether race or individual failing prompted their exclusion. Either conclusion breeds frustration and eventually despair. We call ourselves "African-Americans," but despite centuries of struggle, none of us—no matter our prestige or position—is a few steps away from a racially motivated exclusion, restriction or afront.*
>
> —*Derrick A. Bell Jr.,* Radical Realism

When clients who have experienced racial oppression seek out counseling, they are taking a number of risks. First, these clients must enter a system that exposes them to possible bias, oppression, and misrepresentation. Consider a decision to climb a ladder with the aim to reach a position of safety knowing that the ladder was not built for you or that the destination may or may not be welcoming, especially given all that is required to make the climb in the first place. How can we, as professionals, gain the trust of BIPOC clients in their attempts to utilize a system that has historically caused them more harm than good?

The answer may not be simple, but the first steps seem clear: Acknowledge the past and present practices of discrimination that create harm and reflect the symptoms that are often diagnosed and pathologized in therapy. If we work to move out of the expert role and into one of deep listening and empathy, we set ourselves aside and center our clients in their own lived experience. Nothing can be more powerful in supporting their journey to self-healing than directly acknowledging and collaboratively working to change the systemic practices of oppression. In many cases, our clients' experiences are not our own (and should not be, if we are open to working with a broader representation of humanity), so most of the time, we must start in our own beginner's mind and seek out related resources and education.

One could argue that Western culture operationalizes sexism in a manner opposite that of "color "blindness." The prescribed differences between "the sexes," historically viewed only in the binary of cisgender male or cisgender female, have been heightened to the extremes in ways similar to the binary descriptions inherent in racist ideology existent in White supremacy. However, we are taught to look *for* and *at* gender roles and expectations: how we seek to meet them, where we worry, where we fall short, and so forth. To put it lightly, Freud had a whole lot to say about these supposed unspoken desires and fears related to gender and sexuality, and our field has been looking for those potential connections ever since. We are taught to see gender, for better or for worse, and under a microscope, at that.

Yet not one of us exists solely in our gender or racial identity. We are each breathing representations of unique and complex histories. At the same time, race and gender profoundly impact our experiences in the world and how the world sees and treats us more acutely than other elements of identity. Yet when we sit and consider all that we are, so many pieces make up the complex tapestry of our human existence. Pamela Hays (1996, 2001, 2008, 2012, 2016) has spent much of her career focusing on the various elements of cultural identity and the intersectional experiences that make each person who they are. She has called out the structural power dynamics existent within each of these identity attributes (ADDRESSING model) and highlighted how counselors need to take a more holistic view, not only of their clients, but also themselves and the resulting power dynamics in the counseling relationship. Thus, the counselor must ask, how is the client's presenting problem related to the larger system(s)? Utilizing a feminist approach, the counselor should then look at this "problem" from multiple perspectives rather than the dominant, individual perspective. Context and circumstance are each imperative. With this, a broader frame can be better utilized in finding more authentic solutions unique to a given problem and identity.

Activity: Resilience and the ADDRESSING Model

The model, as presented below, is culturally bound to White, Eurocentric culture, systems, and values. This may look very different from different cultural and social identity locations. It is also crucial that we all consider the intersectionality of our identities. Consider your own addressing model (agent) in comparison to the clients you work with (target). Consider this with your colleague. What is your reaction? In what ways might this inform your understanding of your clientele and colleagues moving forward?

Addressing model	Agent	Target
Age and generational influences	18–65 years old	Younger than 18; older than 65
Developmental disabilities	IQ above 70; no learning issues	IQ under 70; compromised learning; developmental delays
Disability (acquired or congenital, physical, cognitive, psychological disabilities, visible, invisible disabilities)	Able in all areas	Disabilities from injuries, illnesses, or trauma
Dogma (beliefs, philosophy, politics)	Supported by current social values	Different from current social values
Religion and spiritual orientation	Christianity, Christian values, Christian celebrating; no religious preference	Jewish; Muslim; all non-Christian practices
Race (self-identified); uni-, bi-, or multiracial	White	Black; indigenous; people of color; biracial; multiracial
Region (rural, urban, suburban, exurban)	Urban, suburban, exurban (depends on client's location)	Rural (depends on client's location)
Relationship status	Coupled	Single; legally unrecognized relationships; polyamory
Ethnicity: uni-, bi-, and multiethnic	European American; White	Non-European American; unrecognized ethnicities (i.e., those that have faced genocide, loss of identity, etc.)
Socioeconomic status (class)	Middle and high SES	Poverty and low SES; financial dependence; lack of financial support
Sexual orientation	Heterosexual, straight	Lesbian; gay; bisexual; asexual; pansexual
Size	Socially sanctioned weight	Not socially sanctioned weight
Indigenous heritage	Nonnative	Native, indigenous; unrecognized; other
Incarceration	Never incarcerated	Incarcerated
National origin	Born in the United States; United States citizen	Voluntary/involuntary immigration; undocumented; colonial state refugee
Neurodiversity	Neurotypical	Twice exceptionality; overexcitability
Gender	Cisgender men	Women; transgender; intersex; two-spirit; people assigned female at birth; nonbinary; genderfluid; agender; genderqueer; gender nonconforming

(Continued)

Addressing model	Agent	Target
Genetics	Biologically related to parents	Adopted; fostered; step-children
Trauma	No traumatic experiences	Experience of traumatic events; estrangement; disownment; incarceration

Terms	
Agent	People and groups who have initiative, power, and privilege
Target	People and groups who are oppressed and marginalized
Further Information	

Clinician's Profile																
	A	D	D	d	R	r	r	r	E	S	S	I	N	G	g	g	t
Agent																	
Target																	

Adapted from Pamela A. Hays, "Resilience and the ADDRESSING Model," Addressing Cultural Complexities in Practice: A Framework for Clinicians and Counselors. Copyright © 2001 by American Psychological Association.

Community Is Key

How does the client look at themselves within the context of their community? How are they seen by their community, and how do they see themselves in relation to it? There are multiple relational levels that should be considered in our work. Introduced in the 1970s, the ecological framework for human development, described primarily by Urie Bronfenbrenner's (1992) ecological systems theory, postulated that human growth occurs within an ecological system of relational interactions between immediate social (micro), community/environmental (meso), broader socioeconomic (exo), and the beliefs and attitudes of society (macro) systems. This theory of human development set the stage for two related ecological models: the feminist ecological model (Ballou et al., 2002) and the multicultural and social justice counseling competencies (Ratts et al., 2015).

The feminist ecological model describes layers of a person's relational interactions and identity-forming elements. These are biological, emotional and cognitive (individual), relational (micro), institutional (exo), and global (macro) levels existent within climatic and historical contexts, which then inform one's personality and overall view of the self. The goal in this model is to "expose the variety of forces and concerns at play within one's life" (Ballou et al., 2008, p. 62). The counselor is an aid to the client in the process of unfolding those truths and experiencing a truer self, thus behaving, responding, and initiating in more proactive ways (Ballou et al., 2008). Important considerations include:

- Is individual counseling the best or singular course of action?
- Are other or additional interventions more effective/necessary?
- What are the larger group problems in relation to the broader social context?
- What additional solutions might this call for?
- What role does each of those aspects of self and identity play in relation to each aspect of intersection of identity and vis versa? (Ballou et al., 2008, p.63)

As mentioned above, the multicultural and social justice counseling competencies, endorsed by the American Counseling Association in 2015, were also borne out of the ecological, contextual, relational approach. These competencies provide a framework that can be implemented into counseling theories, practices, and research (Ratts et al., 2015). This framework highlights the intersection of identities and the dynamics of power, privilege, and oppression that influence the counseling relationship and include self-awareness, client worldview, counseling relationship, and counseling and advocacy interventions (Ratts et al., 2015).

Recent applications of feminist counseling theory/feminist therapy have been woven into various forms of counseling, such as group counseling and career counseling, where, again, the focus is just as much on the community as it is on the individual. Group counseling seeks to create meaningful relational experiences and reciprocal learning among all who attend the group. It lends itself naturally to the values of feminist ideology—namely, in its illumination of the needs and experiences of both individual voices within the context of the community—with an aim to make invisible aspects of power and privilege visible and, in turn, improve systemic welfare. In more recent approaches to career counseling, clients are again seen first within the context of their community and the expectations placed upon them within these varied roles. In feminist career counseling, the client is no longer simply given a career assessment and sent on their way. These sessions run much more like a combination of strengths-based counseling, narrative counseling, and liberation counseling. Clients' personal situations, relationships, goals, needs, and expectations are discussed in an ecological context, bringing forth a variety of options and considerations for career and educational planning.

Counseling, as a profession, has squarely placed social justice advocacy and multicultural competency at the center of their work. Though debated still, even within our professional membership and governing bodies, this work remains the primary call to action for those in the field of mental health. This means that counselors and related helping professionals must think beyond the one-on-one work that takes place in the counseling office and move it out to the broader community. Here, the concept of community is multidirectional. Community work exists between the counselor and larger local, national, and international groups. There is community work between the client and their immediate social community as well as the larger local, national and international groups. There is community work between each of these groups with one another, collaborating, consulting, unpacking, and reworking. Finally, there is community between the counselor and the client, as each of these individuals inherently represent intersecting identities within this space. Here again, we see how the impacts of presumption, social "norms," acculturated roles, and voice play into our experiences of one another. If we are not careful to see, not careful to listen to, the experiences that are different from our own, we risk furthering oppression through harmful naïveté.

Supporting Our Client's Internal Power

Power is not something that is given or bestowed upon a person with lesser inherent potential for growth or understanding; rather, the counselor is an aid to the person who is in the process of finding their own inherent power. Our job is to carefully and respectfully look at contextual interactions and meaning, systems in play (those that are supportive and those that are oppressive), and the various terrains of the past, present, and future. This work is akin to the Grand Canyon example that Colin provided earlier. We are in the fortunate position of being able to view the elements of a client's lived experience from a distance that gives us, perhaps, a vantage that may be helpful to the client. They are supported in their own journey as we walk alongside them. We do not tell them *what* it is they are seeing, nor do we tell them what their view means. This is the power in their own work. The counselor acts as a partner in the process, believing, with a positivity, that the client's capacity for reaching their more deeply held and embodied self-worth is already in place. The counselor is thus an aid to the client in the process of unfolding those truths and in their experiencing of a truer self. Wholly acknowledging the difficulty in the terrain of the climb, and championing their courage and tenacity to meet the challenges they face. Counselors assist in broadening perspectives by behaving, responding, and initiating in more proactive ways. This includes a noticing of resilient efforts and available strengths. Possibly, these strengths were previously unrecognized (or they have been seen but since pushed down or forgotten) within the experience of familial, social, cultural, and internalized narratives of oppression. Opening space in this way with clients represents the initial seeds toward an increased sense of agency, connection, and contribution and their own expanding consciousness.

Example

In my work as a college counselor, I (Katherine) had the fortunate opportunity to witness the movement of one of my clients from experiencing suicidal ideation and depression to helping develop the campus Safe Space Training Program and first LGBTQ Resource Center. When we first began our time together, Marcus shared with me that he had recently been kicked out of his home. In the preceding week, he had come out to his family, a traditional, Catholic, Mexican American household. Although Marcus was an exceptional student and had received good grades, he was now struggling to show up to class at all. He had been sleeping on his friend's couch for a week and felt an extreme loss in his sense of self-worth. The eldest in a family of four, Marcus had always taken pride in being a watchful big brother, one who set the bar high and helped his siblings with their homework or relational woes. Now estranged from his family, a community that meant everything to him, he no longer felt a sense of life worth.

Our work began slowly, and I remember just being there for Marcus as he would come to my office and break down. He had seen a Safe Space sticker on my door from my graduate program and "didn't know what else to do but show up." This, of course, was everything. In his ability to show up each week, I could see Marcus's resilience. I commended him for it and showed my complete amazement in his strength. Week by week, he shared more about his cultural context, his family, his religion, his community, and, slowly, his goals for the future. At some point, we came to the realization that even though estranged, he could still be the role model for his siblings that he had always been. This reinvigorated him with the hope that one day he might reconnect with his family and be able to show his strength and achievement—two qualities that were highly important to his culture of origin. He began to find his focus in school again, started opening up to friends, and, ultimately, became an incredible activist for LGBTQ rights and support groups on campus. In being true to both himself *and* his community, he was able to let go of much of his internalized negative bias and embrace his true self.

Negative Bias

Traditional personality theories focused on counselor insight and their capacity to "uncover" the client's true self. The self-awareness movement initiated by Freud and expanded on by a variety of phenomenological theoretical approaches—a process once described by Perls (1969, 1973) as the "peeling of an onion"—not only placed the power of the deep dive in the expert hands of another but did so through an exclusive unpacking of negative childhood or historical events. This type of insight work can create what is known as *negativity bias*, where negative experiences, at the neuro-biological level, have a far greater impact than do neutral or positive experiences and will influence how clients respond to counseling (Jones-Smith, 2019). It is far easier to develop feelings of learned helplessness from a few failures than it is to undo those feelings with positive experiences (Seligman, 2002). The general consensus is that it takes five positive lived encounters to overcome the effects of a single negative event (Gottman, 1995). Of course, the more intense the fear and threat of the event, the longer recovery can be for folks in developing a worldview that welcomes personal and social successes. As Jones-Smith (2019) noted, "Clinicians typically seek to confirm negative evaluations with more negative questions, but they typically do not follow up positive evaluations or circumstances with more questions designed to ferret out a clients' positive attributes" (p. 81).

In effect, if both counselors and clients are inclined to gravitate toward a personal and social uncovering of negative self-narratives and related life events, then the deficit conclusions that counselors hold about their clients, and clients about themselves, will remain and likely become exacerbated. As noted in earlier chapters, self-healing is activated by tolerating diversity for both the client and counselor. It is a remembering to the better part of ourselves and positive circumstances "blinded" by the perceptual constriction associated with social and cultural bias and exacerbated by intense affect dysregulation (e.g., anxiety or depression). Clients often see the worst in themselves, in part, because that is how they are perceived by others. If counselors only reiterate and expand on these negative self-evaluations, the client will leave the session with the evaluation of themselves and with the same sense of powerlessness that led them to seek counseling in the first place. In a speech at the seventh annual Women to Women conference, Jessie Potter (1981) was quoted as saying, "If you always do what you have always done, you always get what you have always gotten." Working from the inside out (for both counselor and client), with a rejection to the categories afforded others and a focus on expanding one's view of themselves and the relationships around them, a greater sense of power, agency, and worth becomes far more accessible.

Top Takeaways

1. We wrongly assume that it is our job to "empower" our clients—as though it is a gift that we hold and one that we can choose to bestow.

2. The gaze that clinicians brought to the counseling relationship thus influenced not only how counselors perceived clients but, more importantly, how clients viewed themselves. Instead of focusing on internal strengths and resilience, female clients were encouraged to work on "letting go," "moving on," and reducing expectations.

3. When clinicians are unaware of this bias, they practice in arrogance and judgment, ultimately robbing others of dignity, respect, and resources. The very thing needed for change to occur is the very thing diminished in the process of helping.

4. Resilience occurs via connection to both ourselves and others. It is not that marginalized groups are less resilient; it is that the very nature of their lived experiences reduces access to the conditions where resilience can grow and thrive.

5. The counselor is thus an aid to the client in the process of unfolding those truths and in their experiencing of a truer self. Counselors assist in broadening perspectives by behaving, responding, and initiating in more proactive ways. This includes a noticing of resilient efforts and available strengths. Possibly, these strengths were previously unrecognized (or they have been seen but since pushed down or forgotten) within the experience of familial, social, cultural, and internalized narratives of oppression.

PART II

OPENING SPACE FOR
RESILIENCY AND CHANGE

Resilience-Centered Counseling Relationships

I have been finding treasures in places I did not want to search. I have been hearing wisdom from tongues I did not want to listen to. I have been finding beauty where I did not want to look. And I have learned so much from journeys I did not want to take. ... I am ready to see what really exists on the other side, what exists behind the blinds, and taste all the ugly fruit instead of all that looks right, plump and ripe.

—*Ken Baker (2018, pp. 48–49)*

In our collective years of counseling experience, rarely have clients entered our offices proclaiming that what they wanted most from counseling was to find out more of what was right about them. If only all sessions began like this! More often than not, clients are burdened by what feels wrong, in their lives and in themselves. Symptoms are personalized as reflections of their failings, faults, and struggles as evidence of their weakness. Their stories imply that somehow "I am not strong enough, smart enough, or good enough." They come to counseling seeking relief, with the hope that what is wrong can be fixed. This deficit-saturated narrative has been influenced by trauma, exacerbated by poor attachments, and reinforced by an illness ideology perpetuated in Western medicine: The whole of an individual is dismissed in favor of parsing out specific symptoms. If the right combination of symptoms can be identified, then what is "wrong" can be diagnosed. Client and clinician are now in agreement, where one who perceives themselves as broken seeks another who agrees and prescribes treatment. It is a complementary arrangement that supports an inequity between clients and therapists where clients are described in terms of their limitations and healing as a testament to the expertise of the clinician. The possibility that our clients possess the capacity to heal themselves is abandoned.

This deficit-infused pact between client and counselor is both misguided and tragic. It undermines the role of how clients navigate their own lives in order to cope, survive, and, in some parts of their lives, even to thrive. It also robs counselors of working from a perspective of strengths where symptoms may be less about what is wrong and more about what needs to be right. It is a therapeutic gaze that acknowledges people are far more than the symptoms they describe and far more capable of change than what might seem possible. Too often the inherent strengths of others go unrecognized, unnamed, and unused between clients and counselors. The best in all of us can be shrouded by the difficulty of the next step and the struggle toward a better life. A resilience-centered counseling relationship seeks to shine a light on the strengths, values, and qualities that have been forgotten by time, undernourished by fate, neglected in favor of a more dominant narrative, and sacrificed in an effort to seemingly survive another day. The psychotherapist and client work together to transform suffering into strengths, despair into hope, and loneliness into a greater sense of connection. The first step in this is to take a closer look at what contributes to resilient living.

Decolonizing the Definition of Resilience

Resilience is the result of exposure to extreme stress in response to adverse life events, which provides a shift in perception that allows for a "bouncing back" and an increased tolerance for future challenges. This resilient mindset was initially described as influenced by protective factors. These included being socially responsible, adaptable, and achievement oriented and having a positive outlook and a caregiving environment outside the family (Werner & Smith, 1992). More recently, qualities related to vitality and resilience have been identified, including subjective well-being, optimism, self-determinism, creativity, faith, acceptance, and gratitude. This led to a "strength-based" movement where well-meaning therapists sought to teach and encourage others to be "less of who you are" and shift to being more accepting, forgiving, and self-reliant. Although well intended, it is problematic for a variety of reasons. First, it maintains the counselor in the expert position, where strengths are offered as "preferred" solutions to relieve the suffering of others. It also reflects privilege, implying that if clients had more grit, tenacity, and/or courage, they would become stronger, ignoring the forces of sociocultural oppression influencing their powerlessness. Second, it highlights a view of resilience as a solitary experience rather than an expression of the individual in context, with themselves and the world they live in.

Ungar (2013, 2017) noted it may be that our understanding of resilience is so rooted in this Western-centric, colonial notion of individualism and self-reliance that we are neglecting the wisdoms of non-Western traditions and cultures and missing the opportunity to incorporate them into psychotherapeutic practices. For example, in non-Western cultures, there is generally less separation between the self and others (Kondo, 1990; Rosenberger, 1992), and rather than emphasizing self-determination, collectivist cultures highlight self-sacrifice to the benefit of others (Bell et al., 2004; Iwasaki, 2005). Individuals in collectivist cultures tend to equate harmony with life satisfaction (Kwan et al., 1997), and positive feelings are more rooted in the context of interdependent relationships (Chang, 1988; Markus & Kitayama, 1999). Within more collectivist cultures, a sense of shared efficacy, or communal mastery, may be more central to people's resilience in the face of stress and adversity.

There is a need for a decolonized understanding of resilience, emphasizing not a collection of qualities but rather how self-healing tendencies are activated within caring attachments. These attachments are characterized by respect, collaboration, cohesion, mutual gratitude, and humility. In reference to the counseling relationship, clients are met on equal footing where the emphasis is not on fixing, rescuing, or applying missing attributes; rather, the work rests on a foundation of faith in the client's wisdom and the mutual understanding that suffering witnessed promotes a growing tolerance for dissonant and adverse life experiences.

A New Definition of Resilience

Below are the four features of resilience, representing an arch (see Figure 9.1). The purpose of an arch is to provide a strong and self-supporting opening into a structure. Resilience is supported by four interrelated features of healing: connection, culture, community, and capacity.[1]

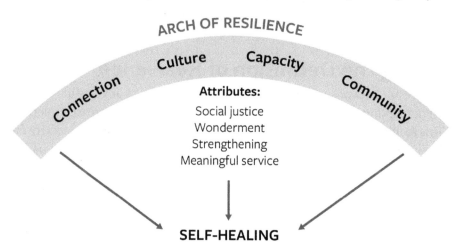

FIGURE 9.1 Arch of Resilience

Connection: Resilient healing is most often activated in the presence of others who are accepting, respectful, and attuned. Being seen, heard, and having these experiences reflected back provides validation of one's innate wisdom. Being fully accepted without the pressure of living up to the expectation of others, provides the space needed to translate suffering into something else. This type of connection embodies a deep faith that others have the capacity for change and renewal. It is inherently respectful, and when the need to rescue is abandoned by counselors, it empowers others to find the best in themselves, as witnessed by a caring support network. By noting the experience of the story rather than the story itself, opportunities for clients to self-soothe emerge. In fact, the space in between is where imagining and multiplicity become possible, and with that comes a broader sense of who people are and wish to become.

Culture: Resilient healing draws on a collective experience of belonging and group inclusion. For example, a prospective study of 103 Native American women conducted by Hobfall et al. (2002) found that participants prioritizing communal mastery experienced less increase in depressive mood and anger when faced with high-stress circumstances than participants who prioritized communal mastery less. Having a positive cultural identity has also been shown to increase feelings of self-worth, self-efficacy, connectedness, and purpose for Indigenous people (EchoHawk, 1997; White, 2000). Isolation is the antithesis of resilience. Assisting others with accessing shared experiences, beliefs,

---

1. Erica Walters and Erika Parker at Antioch University Seattle each contributed to the 4 Cs of Resilience.

and values as characterized by their cultural group provides an opening for individuals to receive and give support.

Community: Resilient healing is other reliant and community oriented. The whole is always greater than the sum of its parts, and individuals stand tall when interconnected and stabilized with others. Community engagement stands up to the fragmentation resulting from trauma experiences, chronic stress, or life adversity that can overwhelm one's ability to cope. It is the power of interconnectedness that allows the growth of one to nurture all. To find community is to find those small threads that bind us to one another, and when woven together, can withstand an enormous amount of pressure.

Capacity: Resilience is characterized by the self-healing capacity available to all living organisms. When confronted with dissonant life experiences and connected through a sense of community and culture, the forces of equilibration open space for renewal, strength, and meaning. Capacity has little to do with solving problems, prescribing treatment, or seeking to benevolently heal another, and more to do with counselors holding space with love and faith so that people may discover for themselves the strength, wisdom, and understanding needed to withstand the oppressive influence of trauma and adversity. To pursue service toward our deepest ideals and the communities in which we live is the quintessence of a resilient life.

Activity: The Miracle Question for Counselors

Milton Erickson (1954) asked clients to describe how they were able to solve their problems upon meeting their therapist at some time in the future. He called this the "pseudo-orientation in time" technique and provided a shift in working with the end in mind. Steve de Shazer (1985) paralleled this idea through the use of a "miracle question" that encouraged clients to imagine a life when the problem was solved and "more on track." Each quickly shifted the frame (i.e., perspective) in order to open up possibilities. Steve deShazer incorporated this into a social constructivist paradigm and used this as a way to quickly shift the conversation away from problem talk (that was just a recursive narrative loop) toward the co-construction of possibility between the counselor and client, thus off ramping the deficit loop into something preferred. The elegance of the miracle question was not in the question itself but in the counselor's ability to encourage clients to keep looking forward toward perceived competence rather than backward toward helplessness.

Below is a miracle question for counselors. It is designed to shift away from seeing clients as victims of their history and prisoners to their symptoms and toward an envisioned stance of experiencing them as capable and resilient. Please reflect on this with pen in hand and note how this influences what you notice in your next client session.

For a moment, consider a current client and how you experience them. Now, as much as you possibly can, imagine that a miracle occurs between now and the next time the two of you meet. In this miracle, you see only the possible in the client. You have an absolute and unquestionable belief in the capability and inner resources of the client. Although hidden previously, in this miracle, all you can see in this client are their undeniable strengths and their efforts in keeping their head above water. You are concerned only with who they are becoming and cannot help but notice the

(Continued)

virtues and values that they have often sacrificed in efforts to reduce their suffering. Finally, in this miracle, you notice only what is right with the client and how you have been impacted by your work with them. A sense of gratitude and humility are far more present in your experience as the miracle of the next session unfolds.

Hold this miracle close and imagine how this would inform how you show up to the next session. How would you experience the client? How would they experience you? What would be different about you? What would be different about your intent and clinical focus? How might this perspective influence your work with others and with yourself? What would be the first sign in your work with others that this miracle is beginning to take hold … even just a little bit?

Resilience can best be understood not as a fixed idea or set of actions but as a divergent landscape of concepts and dimensions harnessed by clinicians to enhance the resilient qualities of themselves and their clients. This is a convergence that looks inward and sees the inherent worth of others—often in ways unimaginable to either the counselor or client. Clients, not counselors, are the experts on their own experiences and the space created through connection can serve as a light when stumbling around in the dark. This is a convergence to the undeniable truth that resilient living cannot occur in isolation, but only in connection with others, and where there is a striving to be of service to one's personal integrity as well as to one's culture, family, and community. In much the same way that our eyes adjust as we look around, so too does activating our natural inclination toward renewal and self-healing. As we focus inward on our strengths, values, and personal qualities, space is opened to see how these insights might be applied as our gaze looks out to the horizon. In fact, the space in between is the space that invites imagination, multiple ways of seeing the world, and a broader sense of who people are and wish to become.

Imagine yourself on a nature walk. Take a moment to look around you; breathe in the fresh mountain air. The forest you see is not simply a collection of trees competing for light. They are connected by a fungal network, silently communicating. When a tree is in distress, electrical impulses are received by the other trees around it; nutrients are shared. They are intricately intertwined and perform an interdependent dance, conversing their needs to one another in a language only they can hear. Trees do not just stand there as Suzanne Simard (2021) argued: They perceive, respond, connect, and converse. In order for young trees to thrive, they must be planted in proximity to other trees, especially elder trees. The elder trees support, reassure, and provide a stability that breathes life into the younger ones. Collectively, they are all connected and devoted to the well-being of one another. Together, they make a forest. Now, move your gaze to the ground beneath your feet. It is the ground that nourishes the trees, and by your presence, it now also nourishes you. It is what caring communities do for each other. Like the trees in this forest, we stand strongest when standing in a grove.

Example

In the early years of becoming a counseling professional (Colin) it was common practice for private, non-profit agencies to accept client referrals from our county's department of health and human services, as they were often understaffed and overwhelmed. I gladly consented to seeing anyone willing to be referred to a new clinician eager to make a difference in their lives. As such, I began working with a mother whose parental rights of her 6-year-old daughter had been terminated due to a drug use history resulting in repeated patterns of child neglect. As I opened her clinic file, sent over from the county prior to our first meeting, it was thick with stories of generational trauma, poverty, and addiction. They described the client as "chronically noncompliant" and that, given her history, the prognosis of obtaining any level of parenting rights was poor and likely beyond their capacity to achieve. After our first few sessions, I was in complete agreement. Regardless of what I did or said, we ended each encounter both feeling helpless to change and hopeless about to what to do next. It was exhausting, and although I genuinely liked the client, I was discouraged and wondered quietly if had what it took to be a counseling professional. By happenstance, the agency was expanding, and my office was moved to the back of the building. As such, I now escorted folks through a maze of hallways. It was during one of these winding walks that I casually asked this client how they were able to arrive at the agency in such a timely manner. In our six or so sessions together, she had never been late nor missed an appointment. She explained how she left the halfway house at 9:00 a.m. to catch the 9:15 a.m. bus to the transfer station, where she boarded another bus at 10:00 a.m. that arrived in time for her to walk the half mile to our agency. This allowed five minutes of breathing room prior to our counseling session at 11:00 a.m. Astonished and speechless, we walked in silence, where upon entering my office, I conjured up a tentative question related to what motivated her to travel two hours up and back for a one-hour appointment once a week. She quickly identified two reasons. One, a stepfather that was briefly in her life, and someone she admired and trusted, considered timeliness an expression of trust to others. Being punctual was her way of showing respect to me as well as honoring the one adult in her life who provided safety and support. It was, in essence, a remembering of something good in their life she wished to keep alive. Two, overcoming current hardships was the price that needed to be paid to have time with her child. The struggle of her recovery and coming to terms with all that had been lost over the years reflected her devotion as a mother. Regardless of how others may have given up on her, she was unwilling to give up on being a parent to her daughter. She said this with unfaltering determination, and for the first time, I listened. I listened to who she was—defined not by the multitude of problems present in her life, but as someone who was respectful, tenacious, and devoted. I listened to how she was perfectly capable of guiding and directing her own life, and by listening in this way in each subsequent session, we both changed. I began to resist the pull of rescuing, soothing, or providing benevolent suggestions, as this only perpetuated the idea that she and others were broken, fragmented, and incapable. I came to realize that the wonder I experienced as we walked down the hallway together was a version of curiosity I hoped to bring to all my counseling sessions. She tapped into and began to trust her internal resources. Although her recovery was still a struggle, it had less influence on the goals she had for herself. During our time together, she acquired visitation with her daughter, and I had the unique opportunity to witness not only the person she was, but also the person whom she was motivated to become.

Top Takeaways

1. Counseling is often a complementary arrangement that supports an inequity between clients and therapists where clients are described in terms of their limitations and healing as a testament to the expertise of the clinician. The possibility that our clients possess the capacity to heal themselves is abandoned.

2. A resilience-centered counseling relationship seeks to shine a light on the strengths, values, and qualities that have been forgotten by time, undernourished by fate, neglected in favor of a more dominant narrative, and/or sacrificed in an effort to seemingly survive another day.

3. There is a need for a decolonized understanding of resilience, emphasizing not a collection of qualities but rather how self-healing tendencies are activated within caring attachments. These attachments are characterized by respect, collaboration, cohesion, mutual gratitude, and humility.

4. The purpose of an arch is to provide a strong and self-supporting opening into a structure. Resilience is supported by four interrelated features of healing: connection, culture, community, and capacity.

5. In much the same way that our eyes adjust as we look around, so too does activating our natural inclination toward renewal and self-healing. As we focus inward on our strengths, values, and personal qualities, space is opened to see how these insights might be applied as our gaze looks out to the horizon.

A Resilient Social Justice Stance

While no one liberates [themselves] by [their] own efforts alone, neither [are they] liberated by others.

—*Paulo Freire (1973, p. 66)*

The Myth of Meritocracy in Counseling

The myth of meritocracy is alive within the counseling profession. We, counseling students and professionals, are taught to conceptualize the client's "issues" through a problematic lens that sees the treatment of individual problems via a set of universal solutions. Underlying this worldview is the assumption that if the client (via the informed counselor) can more clearly understand their problem (i.e., diagnosis), then a prescribed treatment (via the counselor's lens) will solve their issue and, following initial treatment, the client can either self-correct (i.e., become "resilient," show signs of "strength," pull themselves up "by the bootstraps" and out of their problem) or risk continued pathology (i.e., stay "stuck" or remain fearful/ avoidant of change). As a Western bias to the outcomes of counseling, "if" infers that if people were to just try harder or want something badly enough, then they could push themselves to achieve success (McNamee & Miller, 2004). In many ways, this is the notion of the American Dream, yet within this dream is a fatal flaw: Not all individuals are supported equally within the systems of the Western world or, for that matter, in most places around the globe. Those who face challenges and hardships do not do so simply by fault of their own doing. The human experience is much more complicated than that. The reported problems, symptoms, and ruptured relationships that impact how clients see themselves are deeply rooted in these inequities, yet as counselors, they are so often viewed through a lens of perceived motivational failings, psychopathology, or lack of grit.

As described in Chapter 9, many counselors enter the field holding a similar false expectation of their client's reality. They neglect to look at the situational contexts and communities within which the client is experiencing whatever challenge(s) they bring to the work. What if this established equation in our field was turned upside down? What if the assumption began with an already informed client educating the counselor on their social identity and position in order for the counselor to better understand their context? What if the collaboration between client and counselor then sought to collectively hear and navigate the client's present experience? The outcome of the goals for this navigation could then be defined by the client rather than the prescribed treatment. In this dynamic, the client is not left solely to their own devices to either change/succeed or not: The relationship itself becomes responsible for listening, problem solving, planning, and taking action. The client becomes the central voice in deciding what work is to be done, the timeline, the goals, and the outcome measures.

Too often the interventions utilized in counseling to promote therapeutic change assumes that all clients arrive on equal footing. A social justice-oriented stance looks at client resilience first and foremost from a holistic place. While the counselor certainly brings tools (e.g., diagnostic knowledge, theoretical orientation, education, and experience) to the relationship, just as an athletic coach brings knowledge, technique, kinesiology, nutrition, and motivation to an athlete, our work is that of a supporting cast member with knowledge to assist with the challenges ahead.

A good coach does not tell the athlete what their long-term goals should or should not be, label an athlete as simply "ready to be coached" or not, or treat each hindrance to technical performance as "the same as the next." A good coach gets to know the athlete's context and circumstance, sees them for their strengths, listens to where they want to go, helps them establish their own set of goals, and works with the athlete to set a plan in place to get there. Like a good coach, a counselor working from a social justice stance considers the context of a client's life: what community they live in, who is in their support network, and what access they have to fulfilling basic needs. Such context includes their work, past "injuries," how they balance the demands of family, and other personal and relational factors. A good coach understands that the race belongs to the athlete—win, lose, or draw. It is theirs to run. Regardless of the outcome, a coach must have faith in the capacity of those whom they are coaching regarding growth and pain tolerance and a belief that the performance is less about the finish line and more about the running. When this capacity for self-efficacy is experienced by clients through the eyes of an attuned counselor, the belief in oneself may, too, become limitless.

To create this kind of climate requires an intentional collaboration. In her article on "Making Black Lives Matter," Roxane Gay (2016) wrote:

> Black people do not need allies. We need people to stand up and take on the problems borne of oppression as their own, without remove or distance. We need people to do this even if they cannot fully understand what it's like to be oppressed for their race or ethnicity, gender, sexuality, ability, class, religion, or other marker of identity. We need people to use common sense to figure out how to participate in social justice. (para. 12)

The counselor serves as the witness to the progress, strengths, compassion, and motivation of those with whom they are working. Often when clients find their way to seek support, they have lost the capacity for holding confidence in their abilities. They may believe that change is possible but not know where to start. They may hope to find solutions yet are filled with uncertainty about where to seek them on their own. They may have exhausted their known options, may be running out of energy, or may not be able to tease apart the complexities of their experience, emotions, and a desirable path to the future. When clients seek therapists, they often see them as experts and advice givers who can tell them where they have gone awry or how they need to move in order to feel better. Equipped with potential solutions and/or techniques for promoting change, counselors risk oppressing those they wish to serve in the name of "empirically supported treatments." Mental health professionals must embrace each clinical encounter with a beginner's mind, looking at context first and not deficits in need of fixing. They should listen before speaking. Amelie Lomont (2021) wrote the following dos and don'ts for social justice allyship that seem to encompass this spirit:

Dos	Don'ts
• **Do** be open to listening.	• **Do not** expect to be taught or shown. Take it upon yourself to use the tools around you to learn and answer your questions.
• **Do** be aware of your implicit biases.	
• **Do** your research to learn more about the history of the struggle in which you are participating.	• **Do not** participate for the gold medal in the "Oppression Olympics" (you do not need to compare how your struggle is "just as bad as" a marginalized person).
• **Do** the inner work to figure out a way to acknowledge how you participate in oppressive systems.	
• **Do** the outer work to figure out how to change the oppressive systems.	• **Do not** behave as though you know best.
• **Do** use your privilege to amplify (digitally and in person) historically suppressed voices.	• **Do not** take credit for the labor of those who are marginalized and did the work before you stepped into the picture.
• **Do** learn how to listen and accept criticism with grace, even if it is uncomfortable.	• **Do not** assume that every member of an underinvested community feels oppressed.

The Client Is the Teacher

When therapists first sit with clients, they make assumptions. Human nature can provide a problematic path regarding first impressions, judgment, and perception. At times, this helps to keep a person safe by providing quick information that can activate important fight, flight, or freeze responses. Sometimes, these judgements are incorrect: We subconsciously lean into negative biases and stereotypes and thus may cause harm. Studies on implicit response bias show that when meeting someone for the first time, categorical judgements are made in a matter of seconds (Hinton, 2017). Though scholars (from Tajfel [1969] onward to this day) argue if these biases are the outcome of direct experience or misperception, the end point is the same: Bias occurs quickly and by its very nature is reliant upon false information and assumption. From this impression, we create a story in our mind, greatly influenced by societal and cultural stereotypes. These assumptions inform our vision, correctly or incorrectly, and from there we make split-second decisions on what to do, say, think, and feel. Recognizing this natural tendency is an essential feature of counselors working from a social justice framework. It requires counselors to pause, assess their assumptions, and act while accounting for judgment or bias.

Schon (1987) defined this self-reflection process for the practitioner as "knowing-in-action" and explained, "When the practitioner reflects-in-action in a case [they] perceive as unique, paying attention to phenomena and surfacing [their] intuitive understanding of them, [their] experimenting is at once exploratory, move testing, and hypothesis testing. The three functions are fulfilled by the very same actions" (p. 72). Counselors, therefore, are encouraged to reflect in the moment of action in the same way clients are invited to reflect on the emotions, cognitions, and behaviors associated with change. To achieve this, however, practitioners are confronted with a paradox rooted in traditional linear models advocating prescribed and sequential practices. As Schon (1987) eloquently stated, "In order to gain that sense of competence, control, and confidence that characterize professionals, students of professional practice must first give it up" (p. 72). As clients often seek to establish control within an uncontrollable/out of control situation, the illusion that linearity and control will return with more precision is often damaging to client functioning (Brack et al., 1995). Thus, the ability and quality of a counselor to self-reflect and monitor their undue influence is essential in order for the therapist to maintain the open stance necessary to further the client's internal locus of control. This, then, allows the experience of empathy to be self-directed rather than other-directed, for agency to come from within and not be provided by the counselor.

The impossibility of separating a counselor's values from the process of empathy increases the risk that the therapist might violate the therapeutic context by gratifying personal needs. The ethical responsibility of the counselor to provide a safe and trusting environment while encouraging autonomy is a dynamic that requires the counselor to be both aware of and reflective on the impact of their values and needs on the growth and well-being of the client. Bugenthal (1964) described this as "neurotic gratification" and outlined five therapist dynamics that are therapeutically destructive: (a) one-way intimacy, (b) omnipotence, (c) contingency mastery, (d) giving tenderness, and (e) rebelliousness. As a safeguard, counselors must respond with humility and a willingness to engage in continuous self-reflection.

Therapeutic empathy from a social justice stance, therefore, is a reflection of the human encounter rather than a response to a client. Freire (1990) envisioned this process where, "No one can say a true word alone—nor can [they] say it for another, in a prescriptive act which robs others of their words" (as cited in Santamaria, 1990, p. 76). There are a number of helpful conceptualization tools and theoretical orientations that may be helpful guides. As mentioned in Chapter 9, Hays's (1996) addressing model and Ratts et al.'s (2015) MSJCC model both provide ecological frameworks for thinking about context and intersectionality, as well as recommendations for how to approach the counselor–client dynamic. In addition to these, the Jones and McEwen (2000) conceptual model of multiple dimensions of identity provides a dynamic tool for conceptualizing our client's more salient aspects of identity in a specific space and time. The model (see Figure 10.1) highlights various elements and interactions that make up a person's intersecting identities. This model adds a unique dimensionality where the sphere represents the depth of each of these elements and reflect how, at any given point in time, certain aspects of who we are may be more salient, depending on our context and/or circumstance. For example, when taking courses in school, one's student identity may be "forward" while others may move more toward the back of the sphere. The lines in the sphere represent the connecting relationships and interactions between these aspects of what makes us who we are. These models, which are often used to help us conceptualize the client's presenting issues and context, can serve to support the reflective stance of the clinician and the conceptualization of the counseling relationship itself.

The Mirror

The counselor is a mirror. In fact, we strive to carefully hold and reflect as many little refractions of light as possible, from angles that the client may not have ever seen or considered. There is great power in the choice of where and when we choose to hold up those reflections. Our education and experience provide us a method via which we choose do so and instruct us on how to help those images land. This is not a skill to be taken lightly. It takes tremendous courage for a client to look at an angle of their lived experience in a new and unexpected way. Most critical in that dynamic, however, is not the counselor's determination of meaning found within that image. Change and strength emerges when the client finds and voices that meaning for themselves.

Though we often fear "getting it wrong" as counselors, that fear, like so many polarities, comes from a place of care. We wish to ease our clients' suffering and we fear that what we show them may simply "pile on." We fear that they may not be strong enough to handle it. There are moments when the client disagrees with the light fracture we are holding, and this too can be scary to the novice counselor. It is important to remember that these are also moments of clarity, when the voice of the client speaks clearly to push or shift the navigation of the problem. Here, the concept of right or wrong does not really matter. The client has used their voice to speak their truth, and in that, we must simply and humbly hear an underlying motivation to be heard and understood. If we can meet in this place, we will together gain momentum and purpose. The client's voice emerges, and they take ownership of the collaborative process in the room.

This collaboration is essential. It is relational. It is mutually beneficial. It is the connecting element found in life—an ecosystem of support and balance found through mutual respect and care. To speak boldly and simply, this is the role that love plays in the world. It is a force that draws living creatures together through care, compassion, and connection.

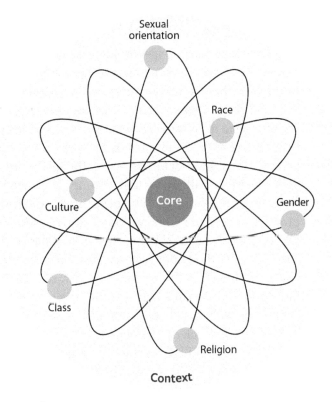

Context:
- Family background
- Sociocultural conditions
- Current experiences
- Career decisions and life planning

Core:
- Personal attributes
- Personal characteristics
- Personal identity

FIGURE 10.1 Application of the Conceptual Model of Multiple Dimensions of Identity
(Susan R. Jones and Marylu K. McEwen, Application of the Conceptual Model of Multiple Dimensions of Identity, from "A Conceptual Model of Multiple Dimensions of Identity," Journal of College Student Development, vol. 41, no. 4, pp. 409. Copyright © 2000 by Johns Hopkins University Press)

Listening to Listen

When we set aside our agenda and seek to listen without changing the mind of the person across from us, we give a gift of love to others. The unique stories of lived experience and what those experiences have to teach us are missed when we are so wedded to our own ideals and, as a result, miss the gift of connection. We, as counselors, should be the *first* to listen. After all, it is what we are trained to do at the core of our work. Listening provides the path forward out of polarized and biased thinking and the harm that results. When we listen deeply, we can hear the unique nuance and texture of another's experience. Though we are faulty beings with taxed systems who also feel and experience daily stress and, at times, our own trauma, we are in the business of leaning in.

Showing up, leaning in, and being open to learning are required attributes of successful helping professionals. In our work, we ask critical questions aimed at making changes necessary to liberate and create more equitable systems—a goal on the horizon that keeps us moving forward. In this, we often are called upon, as social justice advocates, to speak into these spaces of injustice. Our voices are imperative in the journey toward societal improvement, and while we must speak up, our words may also dissipate into the larger conversation. Sometimes (e.g., when too many people are talking without actively listening) these conversations begin to sound like radio fuzz, creating more stress and lack of connection.

Listening is a skill that no doubt brought you to this field. You felt an internal alignment to the work of the helping professional. You took the risk when you joined this profession and bet on yourself that you could provide safety and care for those who are in pain. You have witnessed the process of others—their learning, their growth. At times, that growth may have not been in sync with your own. This is an important reality and a context for bidirectional learning: When we hold space with another human or group of people and listen with humility, setting aside judgment we are also open to our own expansive capacity to learn.

At times, that person is our teacher, supervisor, or mentor. We may see their skills as far beyond our own current capacity. This can be scary or derail us with imposter syndrome if we do not practice humility toward ourselves. We may see their flaws or spaces where their own learning or position has room for further growth. This can also be scary or derail us with distrust if we do not practice humility toward others. In the middle of each of these experiences lies the opportunity to listen. If you think back to your first basic counseling skills class, you can remember the importance of that Rogerian practice of attending. You can remember that stance of holding space with an open heart and mind with the knowledge that, in doing so, we can form a relational bond where trust is established, and authentic reflection and deep learning occurs. This is the work we do in the field of counseling, counselor education, and psychology and in the work of social justice. We create space, we listen without judgment even when we may disagree, and we have faith in the power of healing through human connection.

Activity: Reflective Prompts for Resilient Listening

Reflective practice is a process of "self-supervision" that enables counselors to push for an ever-expanding view of both themselves and those they work with. This involves a willingness to hear not just the story of why people enter the counseling encounter but to grapple with their unique worldview; to acknowledge the inherent hopes and resilient qualities reflective in their struggles; and to consider what this means to both the client and counselor within the space shared. To listen free from the pull of rescuing or healing others is to uplift the client's voice to guide and support their own lives and how they might live with others. With pen in hand, consider a current relationship (e.g., client, partner, friend) and make note of your initial reaction to the reflective prompts in each listening theme (worldview, envisioning, strengthening, experience, and intention). When finished, consolidate your notes into a concise narrative and notice how this experience might influence your next encounter/session with this individual.

Worldview	How would you describe the individual's primary struggle? What might they be experiencing? How do you imagine they interpret the world around them as they go about their day? What do you suppose they whisper to themselves at night?
Envisioning	What do they want most different in their life? What will they need to hold a bit closer for this change to become more alive (e.g., values, strengths, ideas, intentions, interactions)? What might they need to loosen their grip of (sacrifice)?
Strengthening	What sustains them in the face of adversity or emotional distress? Who has influenced the development of these qualities? What does this imply about their most treasured values? If this gets the best of them at times (e.g., overuse), what other qualities might they wish to have available to them?
Experiencing	What is it like to sit in the room with this individual? How would you describe your experience? With their hurt or trauma? What do you know about the individual that that they may not know that you know? How might this be influencing your work with them? What do you wish for yourself as you move forward with this client?
Intentionality	Take a moment to reflect on what you have noted thus far. Check in with your sensations, images, or meanings that seem to resonate with you as you consider this relationship. How might these inform your next encounter/session? What might you need from yourself to continue to stay open to who you are both becoming?

Social Justice in Today's Polarized World

There is so much to say—locally, nationally, and globally—about opinions, experiences, and what comprises our own perceptions of truth. People sit squarely in their own beliefs and experiences: understandably so—what else do we know? While speaking out is critical, voices will continue to swirl with tension and discord in the absence of listening. To courageously speak our truth and compassionately listen are not mutually exclusive practices. We can hold and speak to our experiences, create critical opportunities for change, *and* open our minds and hearts to deeply listen at the same time. As counselors, we are trained to have the humility and the emotional intelligence to sit in that space of duality with both courage and compassion. As humans, we speak out because the visceral memory of how it feels to be heard gives us courage to take that risk. That experience of being listened to is the gift that we bring to your clients and to our world. Listening begets compassion, compassion creates connection, and connection is the first step toward change.

Example

Many years ago, during my Master's in Counseling Program, I (Katherine) was passionate about social justice and had the fortunate experience to be a part of a Safe Space Training Team within my university. As I was preparing to lead my first section of the training, someone dear to me in my life commented on how they hoped that their future child would not identify in the LGBTQ community. We got into a heated discussion, and I ended up walking away in a huff. How could this person say such a thing? I thought that I knew how they viewed the world, and this caused me to completely question both their values and their awareness. Over time, we worked through this conversation enough to where we basically agreed to disagree. Yet, I am sure we both felt hurt by the way we left it. Recently, that same person and I revisited that conversation for the first time in 13 years. She quickly commented:

> I have come a long way—I think differently about that now. But I was also feeling as though, if and when I would become a parent, I might be ill equipped to know how to best support my child were they do identify in a non-binary way. I am still not sure that I know all of the answers, but I know that I could figure it out and that I would love them, no matter what.

As I thought back to my reaction, I recognized my own lack of awareness in our first conversation. I had not really given this person a chance to fully unpack their comment. I had not listened to their experience. Instead, I rushed to judgment and hopped squarely onto my soapbox. If I had slowed down my own reactivity and suspended judgment (ironically, the very thing that I expected this person to do), I would likely have been able to hear that the worry in this person's voice was not simple bias, but a fear of being ill equipped—a concern that perhaps more knowledge was needed than they had in their tool kit. Though those tools may have been in mine, I missed an opportunity to simply sit with this person in community with their experience. Instead, I just ried to force them to hear me--I tried to force my tools upon them. I expected that would create change. Thankfully, thirteen years later, I was given the chance to try it again. I felt deep compassion as I did so, a deeper caring. I hope this time, I heard them.

Top Takeaways

1. Those who face challenge and hardship do not do so simply by fault of their own doing. The human experience is much more complicated than that. The reported problems, symptoms, and ruptured relationships that impact how clients see themselves are deeply rooted in these inequities, yet as counselors, they are so often viewed through a lens of perceived motivational failings or lack of grit.

2. Mental health professionals must embrace each clinical encounter with a beginner's mind, looking at context first, not deficits in need of fixing. They should listen before speaking.

3. Thus, the ability and quality of a counselor to self-reflect and monitor their undue influence is essential in order for the therapist to maintain the open stance necessary to further the client's internal locus of control. This, then, allows the experience of empathy to be self-directed rather than other-directed.

4. This is an important reality and a context for bidirectional learning: When we hold space with another human or group of people and listen with humility, setting aside judgment, we are also open to our own expansive capacity to learn.

5. We can hold and speak to our experiences, create critical opportunities for change, *and* open our minds and hearts to deeply listen at the same time. As counselors, we are trained to have the humility and the emotional intelligence to sit in that space of duality with both courage and compassion.

Surfing

Think of your mind as the surface of a lake or an ocean. There are always waves on the water, sometimes big, sometimes small, sometimes almost imperceptible. The water's waves are churned up by winds, which come and go and vary in direction and intensity, just as do the winds of stress and change in our lives, which stir up waves in our mind. It's possible to find shelter from much of the wind that agitates the mind. Whatever we might do to prevent them, the winds of life and of the mind will blow. You can't stop the waves, but you can learn to surf.

—*Kabat-Zinn (2004, p. 40)*

Critical incident stress debriefing (CISD) was standard practice with assisting survivors of intense traumatic experiences. It was grounded on the premise that expressing the thoughts and feelings associated with the traumatic experience expedited recovery. Early in my career, I (Colin) provided such debriefing services to mental health professionals returning from crisis counseling deployments in response to natural disasters. The sessions were provided quickly upon their return, individually or in small groups, and followed a similar sequence:

1. Introduction Phase (overview to the process)
2. Fact Phase (description of what happened)
3. Thought Phase (exploration of how what happened was interpreted)
4. Feeling/Reaction Phase (allowance for emotional ventilation related to what happened)
5. Strategy Phase (revisiting of predeployment coping skills and stress management tools)
6. Reentry Phase (expression to the experience of the debriefing experience)

Much like the field of trauma counseling at the time, this approach seemed intuitively beneficial. The prevailing assumption was that survivors needed to express their reactions to their experiences. In fact, a refusal to do so might indicate denial and block one's recovery. Furthermore, intrusive memories and other posttraumatic symptoms (e.g., hypervigilance) were considered psychologically distressing at the time and early indicators of posttraumatic stress disorder (PTSD). It was with dismay, then, that I (along with my colleagues) noticed the emerging research on how CISD consistently failed to demonstrate any beneficial outcomes relative to posttraumatic symptoms. In a meta-analysis of CISD outcomes, Van Emmerik (2002) found that not only was CISD no more effective than no treatment at all but also noted evidence that CISD may actually hamper long-term recovery. Cleary, our assumptions about trauma and recovery were mistaken. In his review of CISD outcomes, McNally (2003) proposed that denial might actually be a functional strategy rather than an indicator of pathological avoidance. This new paradigm asserted that people needed time to integrate traumatic experiences, alternating from periods of deep processing to periods of distraction and avoidance. This feel-and-freeze model allowed flashbacks to be processed without overwhelming individuals' coping capacity (feel) while also providing space to focus on the essential tasks of living (freeze). Self-healing was at work, and my work as a benevolent helping professional only got in the way.

The outcome research related to CISD highlighted the natural tendencies to seek balance as well as meaning in the face of dysregulating and traumatic experiences. It also exposed that well-meaning mental health professionals, in their desire to be helpful and reduce the suffering of others, can distract from how suffering triggers the inherent capacity for recovery. Although some level of exposure and integration of traumatic memories has been noted as an essential element in treating trauma (Gentry et al., 2015), clearly it needs to coincide with an individual's own unique pace. This entails conceptualizing avoidance, hypervigilance, and flashbacks as the mind's way toward coming to terms with the incomprehensible. Baron-Cohen (2005) described this as a "mindblindness," where the self is protected from knowing what it is not prepared to know. In other words, avoidance serves as a protective effort to regain some sense of control, and emotional numbing and/or dissociation serve as a deliberate forgetting so that daily obligations can be met. These are not symptoms of psychological distress, but neurological support mechanisms for healing and survival. Another way of thinking about this can be seeing that "shock" has a protective and regulatory function: When pushed out of that state too quickly, we actually destabilize the survivor.

The naturally occurring episodes of freezing and arousal are needed less as individuals become increasingly desensitized to their emotional states, which can usher in the work of integrating dissociated or suppressed traumatic experiences (Siegel, 1999; Gentry et al., 2015). From this perspective, healing is characterized by a gradual embrace and tolerance of the uncomfortable while refraining from turning away. Posttraumatic growth is illustrated by a cognitive rebuilding as people grapple with their new reality (Tedeschi & Calhoun, 2004). Resilience becomes an ever-increasing tolerance to dysregulated emotional and cognitive states as people, families, and communities come to terms with overwhelming events.

Mindful Acceptance

As human beings we have evolved and been conditioned to immediately respond to threats endangering our lives. By anticipating danger and responding to the constant presence of existential threats in our world, the best that life has to offer remains opaque. Furthermore, these threats only need to be found in our memories in order to trigger a response. Our reactions are automatic, powerful, and can defy our best efforts to remain calm. This soothing response is located in our parasympathetic nervous system (PNS) and follows a sympathetic nervous system (SNS) flood of hormones that evoke our flight, fight, or freeze reactions. Although evolved as a way for us to respond to immediate (and anticipated) threats, when people are exposed to repeated threats, abuse, oppression, and trauma, this response system gains strength and begins to dominate the response sets of the individual in such a way as to always keep the person on alert (van der Kolk, 2015). The shift from reactive to restorative mode never occurs. Instead, the stress response (e.g., amygdala), primed for threat, holds the individual in an elevated state of arousal (e.g., stress response, hypervigilance). Without the experience of "bouncing back," regions of the brain needed for restoration, creating meaning, and accessing emotions necessary for resilient and optimal living become unavailable.

In an effort to make room for more delightful experiences, counterconditioning strategies and other interventions have been developed (e.g., stress inoculation). All seem to fall short of the mark. We would suggest that this is because the idea of stopping emotion (perhaps our primary psychic energy source) is doomed to fail from the start. In attempting to make feelings (which encompass SNS and PNS responses) stop happening, we are defying our genetics and evolutionary history. Responses to threats are hardwired to demand our full attention. To ignore them for any significant length of time is quite impossible. This does not mean that alternative experiences, responses, and memories are unavailable, only that they have taken a backseat to a primary or perceived existential threat. A competition of sorts erupts over time where the discouraged person struggles to make feelings that are getting in the way of their life simply go away through some sort of force of will. The problem with this approach is that it sets us up for discouragement. When our SNS is activated, it is a switch that is virtually impossible to turn off. Even when we try to calm ourselves, it might actually create more tension, exacerbating the initial SNS response.

It would appear that perhaps the quickest way to calm an SNS response is to simply not interfere. Fighting it only prolongs the time SNS remains activated. It is very difficult indeed to be calm in the middle of a fight, though not impossible. Once accepted, we make available our other capacities, and PNS will eventually activate. It is designed to follow the SNS response, providing a pathway to a calmer state. Just as more effort and force applied to an SNS response has a tendency to enhance the SNS response, a similar approach to the PNS response is also available. An example of this would be to shift our available focus to other memories associated with feelings of stillness and wellbeing in an effort to activate the PNS. When we recall memories of danger, we trigger our SNS even though the situations remembered are not occurring now. The same happens when we recall pleasant experiences. All the good feelings we had at the time emerge once again. Practicing this enhancement for pleasurable experiences is not something most of us are taught to do or even know about. Yet we get plenty of practice with the threat side of things. By accepting the nature of our stress response, which is designed to save and protect us, while also holding close those experiences of pleasure and agency, we activate a neurobiological response designed to restore balance. It is the nature of all things and an essential element of healing and resilient living. The activity below is an example of this kind of remembering.

Activity: Inoculation

Inoculation is a reflective experience to stimulate an intentional neurobiological response in the face of stress inducing situations. The steps below are designed to increase self-confidence, highlighting an invitation to one's "best self" in resistance to anxious and worrisome thoughts. It is the development of a mindset that empowers one to be in greater service to a set of personal strengths and values rather than in reaction to stress-inducing situations or interactions.

STEP 1: Grounding
- Bring attention to your breathing. It can open space in recognition of the moment, and as this occurs, pay attention to any thoughts or images that might arise. Be attuned to the idea of "letting go and letting in."
- Briefly notice the relaxing sensation of the air traveling back and forth though your nasal passage and how this allows other parts of your body to do the same (e.g., shoulders).

STEP 2: Witnessing
- Imagine a situation where you wish you could have a greater sense of freedom in your response to worry, anxiety, and/or fear. Witness, in your mind's eye, the impact that this trigger situation has on your experience:
  o What do you feel (physical tension/sensations)?
  o How do you feel (emotional responses)?
  o What images and thoughts were weaving in and out (self-narrative)?
- Be sure to *pause* before your thoughts/feelings escalate to the worst-case scenario.

STEP 3: Holding
- Imagine your better self:
  o Imagine what you would like to remember about yourself. What strengths will you apply (e.g., openness, optimism, honesty) that will be more in service to your personal values (e.g., kindness, compassion, contribution)?
  o What compassion for yourself would help to keep your anxious thoughts at bay? What do you notice (ideas, feelings, sensations) as irritation and worry have less of a hold on you? What wisdom does this carry for you?
  o (Option for relationships): How can you remember that the best way to reduce interpersonal conflict is to hold space for multiple perspectives rather than only your own, which can lead to blame and resentment? Express what is true for you and allow the other to do the same.

STEP 4: Reflect
- Focus on slowing and reflecting on the mindset, as noted above. Imagine being more in service to this mindset rather than in reaction to the situation or others.
- Resist the impulse to blame (the other or yourself). Stay open to diverse perspectives as you reflect on staying conscious of your best self.

STEP 5: Apply
- Ground, witness, hold, and reflect as much as possible during the week. This can be done in *quiet contemplation or in movement* (e.g., walking, hiking, listening to music, or other

(Continued)

creative activities). To remember the better parts of ourselves is to inoculate present and future stress-inducing situations. This is the foundation for resilient living.

- Notice situations where you feel the pull of self-protection as well as opportunities to apply a mindset that allows for increased degrees of personal and professional confidence.

- Identify small ways in which to apply this mindset at work and home. Make note (without self-judgment) of those actions and attitudes that might need revising.

- Finally, to pause and reflect on how our better selves can be more present in stressful situations is to employ the power of mind-body medicine. We become what we predict. To inoculate oneself against the neurobiological reaction to high levels of anxiety and fear is to bring increased access to executive brain function: an intentional response in service to a preferred mindset rather than in reaction to a protective stress response (i.e., flight, fight, and freeze).

Tapping into Vitality

Recall a moment of recent pleasure or vitality when you felt the energy of being closer to your better self. Savor the moment, and with pen in hand, reflect on the following prompts:

- What feelings were more alive with you?
- What seemed more open to you?
- What was alive in you that others might have witnessed during this moment? What did they receive from you and you from them?

Now scan your body, arms, legs, and hands. Now your face, jaw, neck, and shoulders. What sensations are present? How has the felt sense of your body changed? What ideas about yourself seem more present? Notice your breathing and allow your attention to return to the present. Linger in the moment and consider what part of this experience you might wish to keep close in the days ahead. Imagine how this might influence how you hold yourself and the parts of yourself that might be more available to others. Imagine this with as much detail as you can and ask yourself a final question: Is this something I want more of for myself and in my relationships?

Recalling our lived experiences of vitality account for some interesting outcomes. When activated, these assets can prevent negative self-appraisal of stressful events, counterbalance more negative emotions, and assist with adapting to and coping with challenging life situations (Masten, 2011; Fletcher & Sarkar, 2013). A dose of positive affect can restore capacity for self-efficacy and willingness to exert control (Tice et al., 2007). Larkin's (2003) study showed that resilient individuals fostered positive emotions that correlated with response patterns in the right thalamus and the inferior and middle frontal gyri—all of which are responsible for regulating emotions. In fact, Davidson (2012), in their study of trauma, suggested that accessing positive affect stimulates the left prefrontal cortex in such a way that the usual stress response of the amygdala was inhibited, thereby shortening the time for recovery. As the gatekeeper of how we react to stress (e.g., flight, fight, or freeze), the amygdala knows nothing of reason or has access to cognitive functioning. As a small, almond-shaped portion of the brain, the amygdala is driven by fear, rage, and despair and, when activated, can be overreactive and literally freeze the ability to think. Individuals with PTSD have been shown to have overly active amygdalae (Shin et al., 2006). Fostering positive emotions counterbalances the neurobiological effects of stress while enhancing emotional self-regulation and the ability to actively cope with tough life experiences.

Fredrickson (2002) studied the characteristics of resilience-oriented people and found that although they still felt as many of the negative emotions as others, it was the positive emotions that accounted for their ability to rebound from adversity, ward off depression, and continue to grow. It was not the absence of fear, anxiety, or sadness but the addition of something else that buffered the negative effects of adversity: a remembering to what feels good rather than avoiding that which does not. The ability to remember, to hold space with the uncertainty, the self-reassurance, positive sensations, and the somatic calm needed to tolerate ambiguity, can open space for new meanings. Although a sense of self-competence can be lost in response to acute trauma, when intentional awareness is focused on internal sensations, self-regulation and access to positive internal resources can occur (Nummenmaa et al., 2014).

What does all this mean? A therapeutic conversation that embodies client strengths can provide a pathway to an emotionally positive experience that results in somatic calming. The PNS, responsible for lowering the effects of stress (e.g., cortisone), can be activated by a shared therapeutic dialogue focused on client strengths, values, and positive emotions. Vitality is ever present and reflects an enduring quality that embodies the capacity for both living and growth. It fuels possibility and lifts up the better parts of ourselves. It allows people to step back and consider not just what is happening but who they wish to become. This is the essence of resilience-centered counseling: to engage others in the pursuit of their "better angels" and to recognize strengths, identify values, and be in service of the growth of both.

To develop resilience, therefore, is neither an avoidance nor a forgetting. It is not making lemonade out of lemons or a constructed truth with the hope of feeling better. Avoidance is isolating. It separates us from the truth and ourselves. It is embodied by shame that undercuts our ability to connect with others or address future adverse experiences. Resilience is the recognition that pain, adversity, and trauma are not reflections of who we are but simply what happens as part of the human experience. Hence, resilience is not the absence of these experiences but the emergence of something new: new ways of knowing that increase our connection to others as well as ourselves. Resilience is an honest appraisal of what happened, the courage to acknowledge the power of the event and its impact, to seek balance when unbalanced, to integrate toward something new. Surfing takes strength, balance, awareness, appreciation for the wave, and the awareness that fighting it will not work. The surfer is never stronger than the wave, but they can learn to ride along with a unique mix of confidence and humility.

Top Takeaways

1. This new paradigm asserts that people needed time to integrate traumatic experiences, alternating from periods of deep processing to periods of distraction and avoidance. This feel-and-freeze model allows flashbacks to be processed without overwhelming individuals' coping capacity (feel) while also providing space to focus on their essential tasks of living (freeze).

2. Posttraumatic growth is illustrated by a cognitive rebuilding as people grapple with their new reality (Tedeschi & Calhoun, 2004). Resilience becomes an ever-increasing tolerance to dysregulated emotional and cognitive states as people, families, and communities come to terms with overwhelming events.

3. It would appear that perhaps the quickest way to calm an SNS response is to simply not interfere. Fighting it only prolongs the time SNS remains activated. It is very difficult indeed to be calm in the middle of a fight, though not impossible. Once accepted, we make available our other capacities, and PNS will eventually activate.

4. When we recall memories of danger, we trigger our SNS, even though the situations remembered are not occurring now. The same happens when we recall pleasant experiences. All the good feelings we had at the time emerge once again. Practicing this enhancement for pleasurable experiences is not something most of us are taught to do or even know about.

5. A therapeutic conversation that embodies client strengths can provide a pathway to an emotionally positive experience that results in somatic calming. The PNS, responsible for lowering the effects of stress (e.g., cortisone), can be activated by a shared therapeutic dialogue focused on client strengths, values, and positive emotions. Vitality is ever present and reflects an enduring quality that embodies the capacity for both living and growth.

Wonderment

Wonder is the beginning of wisdom.

—*Socrates*

Wonder is that feeling of surprise mixed with curiosity often caused by something beautiful or unexpected. *Curiosity* stems from the Latin root *cura*, meaning to "handle with care," and highlights a desire to know or learn something extraordinary (American Heritage Dictionary, 2009). *Wonderous curiosity*, therefore, is a willingness to enter the extraordinary world of another without judgment or agenda while standing in awe of their beauty. There is an old folk tale of a student who, in seeking wisdom from a master, was asked if they would care for tea. As the master poured, the tea began to spill over the brim of the cup and onto the lap of the student. The student cried out, "The cup is full," and the master quickly replied, "As are you." Wonderous curiosity requires counselors to suspend all they know and to first "empty their cup" so that they might engage others from a place of not knowing to experience the other fully for who they are without bias or judgment but with curiosity and unconditional wonderment. It is a commitment to experience others for the first time, every time.

This type of listening represents a decision to suspend personal values in order to walk alongside this person, our client. We attempt to see what they see while reflecting back what we see in their strengths. Implied within the fact that there exists a struggle, we can also infer that hope exists within their conflict. There is energy there, be it exhausted, confused, angry, sad, depressed—these are natural reactions to a struggle and are evidence that hope sits deep within it. Described as being in a "not-knowing" position by Anderson and Goolishian (1992), the therapist communicates an abundance of genuine curiosity where

> the therapist's actions and attitudes express a need to know more about what has been said, rather than convey preconceived opinions and expectations about the client, the problem, or what must be changed. The therapist, therefore, positions himself or herself in such a way as always to be in a state of "being informed" by the client. (p. 29)

It is not a passive position, but an active gaze that notices the space between the lived experiences so that the rest of the story can be told: to notice strengths where only deficits are expressed, to see preferences in life's problems and anticipation where there is resistance, and where despair resides, to see that hope lives there as well. Our clients often enter counseling fatigued with a weariness resulting from the tireless efforts in managing life's stress, challenges, and marginalizing experiences. This constant exertion can impact concentration, mood, and our ability to fight off disease as well as cope with unforeseen occurrences. In this way, fatigue is a statement about the difficulty of the climb and not the climber. It is not an estimation of an individual's level of functioning in terms of presenting problems and personal deficits but rather an understanding of those adaptations needed to survive. To listen with wonderment is to hear how anxiety and depression are reflections of reasonable reactions to unreasonable demands and how motionlessness is a response to trauma, adversity, and oppressive forces. Keeping one's head above water is often a heroic act given the strong currents below. Life is difficult, and as Scott Peck (1978) noted, this is one of the great truths that, once accepted, can be transcendent. Struggle is a reflection of this truth and defines the strong current of the water and the winding shape of the shoreline. As counselors, we must not confuse clients' emotional, cognitive, and behavioral distress with their resilient efforts. Life is difficult, and most are doing the best they can to not let the "road less traveled" get the best of them.

An Active Gaze

Mosaic art is just like life. There are pieces put together and some of the pieces are broken. Life is the same, the pieces are like stages in life, and the broken pieces are like calamities. Although they are broken and torn, if glued together and take a step back, it is a piece of beautiful artwork. In life, if we can appreciate the meaning of the so-called negative events, we will realize that our life is as beautiful and multifaceted as a mosaic art.

—Chi Ying S.I.

Judith Herman (1997), in her work on psychological trauma, concluded that the symptoms of hyperarousal, intrusion, and constriction were not pathological but a description of adaptive responses to the unthinkable. Following traumatic events, the human systems go into a readied state of self-preservation. Cortisol—the essential stress hormone that prepares the body to fight, flee, or freeze—levels are higher in survivors of sexual abuse than control groups who had not experienced such trauma (Lemieux & Coe, 1995; Heim & Nemeroff, 2001, 2008; Bremmer, 2003). As such, the restorative elements of our stress response system that make the body less reactive to stress cues cannot be activated. This has the effect of holding individuals in elevated states of arousal, and without the experience of "bouncing back," critical regions of the brain needed for processing experiences, creating meaning, and accessing emotions necessary for resilient living are unavailable. Levine (2003) noted that the human response to a perceived threat is biological, primitive, and instinctual, wherein an array of multisensory reminders (i.e., smells, sounds, and images) can trigger a stress response and derail one's sense of well-being. Neuroimaging has shown that as people are overwhelmed with stress, fear, and anxiety, the brain areas most involved with formal cognition are deactivated (van der Kolk, 2013). So rationality, the very thing needed to put the fragmented pieces of life events together in meaningful ways, is absent.

The reason many clients stumble when asked to explain their overwhelming anxiety, fear, or depression is not that they do not or cannot know; they just do not have access to those areas of the brain to help with knowing. By noting the experience of the story rather than the story itself, wonderous curiosity provides those opportunities needed for the self-regulation necessary in transforming helplessness into patterns of personal agency and resilience. To be focused on one's experience of events winnows the details so that only the person remains. It is calming to be seen not as damaged, broken, or ill but as remarkable and unique. Aspects of this essential resilient gaze are a focus on the immediate as well as the space in between what is known and that which is still unknown.

Appreciation to the Struggle

Staying curious to how people have been "stretched" by life's adversities and wondrous to those resilient attributes necessary in one's fight for freedom is the essence of a resilience-centered stance. If people are far more than the problems expressed on their intake sheets, then the struggle itself becomes an invitation to the very best of oneself. The gaze of the counselor becomes less about the client story itself and more about how the story defines the storyteller: an attunement to what is being experienced of what is being said. Too much emphasis on the past (e.g., regret) or the future (e.g., worry) only serves to reinforce the implication that life has more control over our experience than we do. The brain and our ability to process experience performs far more efficiently when noted in the present (i.e., keeping the end in mind by minding the present). Practicing and utilizing first-person struggle reflections will assist with establishing a shared understanding of the client experience of a story as they are experiencing it. It is literally reflecting back to others your best guess about what they might be telling themselves in reference to the problems or distress they are expressing and then inviting them to clarify. This type of reflective listening is designed to (a) shift the shared dialogue from the facts of the story to how the story is being self-narrated in the moment and (b) attune toward how clients see themselves, who they hope to become, and how the struggle is informing them on what they desire (e.g., acceptance, belonging, competence). An example might be a reflection of wonder back to the client:

> I wonder if what you say to yourself is "I am afraid to say how I feel for fear that I might be judged or ridiculed. Better to keep things inside, even if it means keeping people at arm's length. My depression is a reflection of these efforts to stay safe at all costs." How does that fit with what you are experiencing right now?

People are constantly narrating interpretations of themselves, and rarely pausing to consider the impact these stories have on themselves. Clinicians who become preoccupied with deconstructing the details within client stories of suffering will ignore the suffering before them. The first step in resilience-centered counseling is to recognize and reflect the debilitating narratives that rob clients of the agency they desire most. These narratives are often whispers of defeat in the face of adversity. To remain curious about their history and the influence these ideas have on clients; to explore together the sacrifice required to keep these ideas alive; and to identify the forces responsible for their protective nature and the daily emotional toll of those forces is to open space for something else. It is empowering to acknowledge that which seeks to define ourselves as powerless. People are far more than the stories they tell themselves, and by recognizing their influence, counselors and clients reduce the strangle hold of these narratives, opening space for the strengths and personal attributes of survival present in clients all along.

Life is far too complex to be seen in binary ways, and clients are far more remarkable and interesting than the histories they share in counseling. Miller and Rollnick (2002), in their seminal work on the tenets of motivational interviewing, described *ambivalence* as a normal reaction to the human experience when balancing "the need to do something different" with "the benefits of doing more of the same." They contended that it is not the absence of ambivalence that embodies wellness but the presence of it. This perception can be heard in the experience of clients as they describe a reluctance to sacrifice the known for the unknown, the resignation that change is hopeless, the rebellion that change would be a "giving in" to another's demand, and/or rationalization of how change, although needed, is unlikely given the current state of things. A gaze of wondrous curiosity appreciates the importance of life's struggles where wellness is more than the absence of disease and meaningful self-discovery and relationships cannot be fully achieved by merely replacing an unwanted thought or behavior.

To appreciate the multiplicity of a lived experience is to focus less on the story and more on how the struggle itself (rather than the problem) highlights the often-impossible demands faced by many. In addition to first-person struggle reflections is the use of both/and reflections. Desiring something different in the face of life's challenges implies the sacrifice of something already known. The pull of the status quo can be as strong as the hope for change. Both are true. We can love and hate someone at the same time where indecisiveness is less about one's problem-solving skills and more about the struggle in deciding on a course of action where each future option is true. There exists an upside and downside on each path forward, depending on your view. Both/and reflections note the multiple truths on the plate of others while wondering on the impact of experiencing such a struggle for so long:

- So, it sounds like maybe you know and do not know: "that I am often not in control of my emotions, and I know that forcing myself doesn't work in feeling better." What is this like to balance these two experiences?

- So, maybe, in many respects, you have both your foot on the gas and break simultaneously: "The only way I know to feel better is to work longer and harder, even at the cost of my health and relationships. I want to be competent and exert control over my life, and I desire increased moments of calm. The holding of one negates the holding of the other." Is that close to your experience? In what ways has this struggle taken control of your life? What are you noticing now that we share this with another?

The stories that clients express with regard to their struggles are purely a conduit in better understanding the impact of their lived experiences: how they are feeling, what the story means about themselves and their relationship with others, the strengths needed to keep things from getting worse, and the sacrifice associated with every choice. Since free will comes with a cost, focus on what the story implies about the storyteller's values, grief, and aspirations (in the moment in which they tell you). These are their stories of becoming: becoming more accepting, more aware, more connected, and stronger. People get to be the experts of their lives and the heroes of their own stories. What do they whisper to themselves in the darkness before sleep? What fears surface as change is considered? What hopes have been sidelined in order to meet other priorities? What is being sacrificed to keep the status quo? And what strengths lie in waiting for the courage needed to be resurrected? Listen not to the story of events or the experiences of others, but to their stories of who clients are and are becoming. The counselor attribute of wondrous curiosity is demonstrated by an attunement to the struggle: a shared understanding of the client's somatic experience, disruption to the status quo, emotional impact of the struggle, and the values or preferences being sacrificed in light of the current struggle.

Somatic Experience

In the moment when people share their struggles, they are, in many ways, also reexperiencing the troubling events of their lives. This is often expressed somatically through changes in vocal quality, posture, breathing, and facial and body tension. As noted by Sharon Stanley (2016), the practice of

---

Activity: A Resilience-Centered Approach for Deconstructing Narratives

Shared understanding between clients and counselors becomes less about the story itself and more about how the story defines the storyteller: an attunement to what is being experienced of what is being said. The following sets of questions are designed to develop a case narrative illustrating the client experience in counseling. The focus questions can be used to broaden the counselor's perception of client experiences or can be shared with clients to assist with broadening their perception of themselves.

Struggle Perception

- Describe the client's perception of their hurt. What might they call it? What is the client's theory about how the hurt developed and why change has proven difficult?
- What impact is this having on them? In what ways does the "long arm of the past" take hold of the client?
- Describe the emotional impact this struggle with hurt is having on them. What does the hurt secretly whisper in the ear of the client?
- In what ways is the client attached to the hurt? What would be compromised if the client decided to think differently about the hurt?
- What is the hurt/trauma event robbing from them? What is being sacrificed? What personal hopes are being dashed or diminished?

Resilient Efforts

- What is sustaining them in the face of their struggle with hurt? Describe the "rest of the client story" about how they keep hurt from taking over.
- How would you describe the client's better self? In what ways is their better-self compromised in the context of their struggle?
- Describe the client in reference to the 4 Cs of resilience:
  - connection to a caring support network
  - cultural identity of shared experiences, beliefs, and values
  - community engagement and service to values beyond the self
  - capacity for tolerating dissonance, ambiguity, and multiplicity
- Imagine a time in the future when you and the client meet:
  - What will they be sharing about what they learned, about others and relationships, and about their hopes for the future?
  - If you were to believe this to be true for the client, even just a little bit, how might that change your interaction with them?

witnessing the moment-to-moment activity of the body from the vantage of the cerebral cortex—or, as noted earlier, stepping back from the chalkboard—makes it possible to see dynamics in ourselves that have been unconscious, dissociated, or unavailable for observation or modification. To assist, Stanley encourages counselors in the practice of *somatic inquiry*, a curious and respectful wondering to the inner world and lived experiences of others. It is a mindful and gentle way of acknowledging arousal, in any given moment, so that new perspectives regarding life events might occur. Somatic inquiry can be used to broaden awareness in reference to life struggles (e.g., "I can hear the impact of your current struggle and am wondering what you might be noticing in this moment") as well as to moments of vitality (e.g., "When you recall time with your son, your breathing appeared to slow, and you sat back in the chair. What are you noticing in this moment?"). An attunement to the body can provide a window into the inner narratives of others, provide an empathic connection as a shared experience between two people, and, finally, increase a willingness and tolerance for uncomfortable sensations (Stanley, 2017). It is not the dissonance of life that defines a resilient mindset but how we "hang on" to the better parts of ourselves in the midst of the dissonance.

Disruption of the Status Quo

As noted in previous chapters, there is a natural movement toward balance in the face of disruption. Wonderment is the attunement to those efforts seeking to reestablish stability and a lessening to the chaotic experience associated with adversity and the contemplation of change. These initial efforts toward healing represent a push back against the experience of distress, pain, and chaos. At first, the benefits of the known and familiar can far outweigh the benefits of embracing the unknown and the unfamiliar. Counselors with wonderous curiosity understand the normality of this resistance and how it can be protective from fear and worry. Bill O'Hanlon described providing a reflection of understanding with a slight twist. The intent is to affirm the client's conclusions and then add an opening (or twist) that shifts away from powerlessness toward a personal agency. For example, I (Colin) once reflected back to a client:

> You may be right that an opportunity for becoming a better you was, in your words, sabotaged. I wonder if your conclusion is that even though you didn't know this at the time, you got in your own way of becoming the person you hope for yourself today. Maybe the older you in this moment has a perspective (some might say wisdom) that was likely less available to you then than it is today. I am wondering your reactions to this as well. If part of this might be true for you, what that might mean as you consider yourself moving forward?

Respect, responsibility, and humility are all features of a resilient mindset. We all seek faith in ourselves, in our capacity to navigate the troubled waters of adversity. As lifelong commitments, we are all unfolding and will fall short, a process nurtured by grace and strengthened by the light of our better selves. Appreciating how individuals have been stretched by life's struggles allows a window into those resilient attributes necessary in one's fight for freedom and agency.

Impact of the Struggle

At its core, the therapeutic relationship is an action of transparency: the transparency of the counselor to demonstrate sincere acceptance, support, with an invitation toward self-discovery and the transparency of clients to recount their stories of distress with an empathic stranger while exploring the impact and influence life problems are having on themselves and others. Below are prompts designed to better understand how client struggles have been impacting and influencing their lives and themselves. They seek only to engage both parties in understanding the impact and influence persistent struggles and oppressive forces are having on clients' lives as well as their expectations for counseling. It provides a foundation for appreciating the distinction between life problems and the unique qualities of individuals and families struggling for "better lives." Examples include:

Impact	Influence
• What impact has this struggle had on you/others?	• How does the struggle influence how you think about yourself? What does it whisper in your ear?
• How has it robbed you of what you want?	
• How does it get the best of you? What has it promised you?	• How much of your life does it control? What will you notice about yourself when you are getting the upper hand?
• What do you think will happen if you do not make a change?	• Who else might be an advocate with you in standing up to the influence of the problem?

Sacrifice (Preferred, Values, and Becoming)

There is a story of an individual that climbs a steep mountain in search of a wise elder to answer how to attain happiness. After an arduous journey, they find themselves sitting before the wise elder, and upon hearing the traveler's request, the elder briefly responds, "And what are you willing to give up to make this possible?" Every struggle represents a grappling of holding on to something at the expense or loosening of something else. What fears surface as change is considered? What hopes have been sidelined in order to meet other priorities? What is being sacrificed to keep things from getting worse? And what strengths lie in waiting for the courage needed to be resurrected in order to tolerate the discomfort and change? Therefore, stories of resilience are stories of becoming: becoming more accepting, more aware, stronger, and more connected. It means listening not to the story of events or the experiences of others but to their stories of who clients are and what they may need to let go of in order to open space for the preferred.

• **Sacrifice example:** "I notice that this struggle is robbing you of the kind of relationship you have always wanted with your sister: one of friendship. What else is this struggle robbing you of?"

As noted previously, if the goal of counseling is to assist others in withstanding and soothing themselves in the face of overwhelming stress and life events, then to do this for them is to imply that they cannot do this for themselves. Assisting clients to work from the bottom up with somatic and affect regulation is not only best practice but also illuminates the power of mind-body medicine. By noting the experience of the story rather than the story itself, opportunities for clients to self-soothe will emerge. In fact, the space in between is the space that invites imagination, multiple ways of seeing the world, and a broader sense of who people are and wish to become. Acceptance and gratitude reside in the right hemisphere and, when acknowledged, has been demonstrated to reduce worry and increase self-narratives of efficacy or competence (Davidson, 2012).

Top Takeaways

1. Wonderous curiosity requires counselors to suspend all they know and to first "empty their cup" so that they might engage others from a place of not knowing, to experience the other fully for who they are without bias or judgment but with curiosity and unconditional acceptance.

2. Neuroimaging has shown that as people are overwhelmed with stress, fear, and anxiety, the brain areas most involved with formal cognition are deactivated (van der Kolk, 2013). So rationality, the very thing needed to put the fragmented pieces of life events together in meaningful way, is absent.

3. Too much emphasis on the past (e.g., regret) or the future (e.g., worry) only serves to reinforce the implication that life has more control over our experience than we do. The brain and our ability to process experience performs far more efficiently when noted in the present (i.e., keeping the end in mind by minding the present).

4. There is a natural movement toward balance in the face of disruption. Wonderment is the attunement to those efforts seeking to reestablish stability and a lessening to the chaotic experience associated with adversity and the contemplation of change.

5. Therefore, stories of resilience are stories of becoming: becoming more accepting, more aware, stronger, and more connected. It means listening not to the story of events or the experiences of others but to their stories of who clients are and what they may need to let go of in order to open space for the preferred.

Strengthening

Effective counseling is about engaging people in the re-authoring of the compelling plights of their lives that arouse curiosity about human possibility and in ways that invoke the play of imagination.

—*Michael White (2007, pp.75–76)*

Strengths are the imperceptible intentions for a better life that go unnoticed due to the noise and urgency of living. Life's storms can narrow perception and quickly generate a cycle where fear begets fear, and the experience of anxiety serves only to highlight worry and dread. White and Epston (1990) described this pattern as a problem-saturated story where individuals perceive, anticipate, and act on only those experiences consistent with their personal "narratives." Strengths, therefore, are not to be confused with merely wishing away problems or the creation of new fictions. They are not simply finding positive qualities generated from negative experiences (false reassurance) or providing clients with counselor-generated affirmations (a hoped-for truth). Strengths are not qualities that we provide others, as this would reflect more about the counselor's need to comfort than the client's need to be comforted. Rather, they are emergent truths reflected in our struggle to heal, overcome, and find meaning. Strengths are often an unrecognized commitment of personal, relational, physical, and spiritual survival. They reflect qualities hidden by a sacrifice of one value for another and efforts to "right the ship" while "keeping our heads above water" when overwhelmed. They are often hidden from our own view, as we work to simply survive in life. The last thing we tend to do as humans is stop and soak in our strengths in the face of challenge. The challenge is usually pretty loud.

From this gaze, strengths are an inherent feature of suffering. They exist simultaneously, where the embrace of one provides an opportunity to embrace the other. The events of adversity and trauma cannot be rewritten. They are the hard truths of the human experience, and bouncing back from these lived experiences is not about "making lemonade out of lemons." People are far more than their history and are defined not by what has happened, but by a recognition of who they are and what they hope to become. Where there are perceived deficits, there are strengths; where problems arise, there are preferences; where there is resistance, there is also anticipation; and where there is illness, there are opportunities for wellness. Irv Yalom (2008) contended that by "staring into the sun" of our own mortality, anxiety gives way to appreciation. Lent (2004) argued that counseling can be conceptualized as an enterprise designed to restore well-being. By focusing on the struggle against daily problems rather than just the problem and/or solution itself, the dynamic qualities of personal resiliency can be explored. Within these efforts of resiliency are strength attributes that can be understood and utilized by clients in seeking symptom relief as well as a restoration of life satisfaction. Resilience, then, is a process of strength development and the personal witnessing of this development. It is often a remembering of the better parts of ourselves forgotten over time, clouded by adversity and hidden by fear and shame. The struggle against life's adversities has little to do with feeling better and more to do with seeing for ourselves that we are strong and can grow stronger. Counselors do not give others strength but provide a calming setting to uncover those attributes awaiting to be seen and to be seen with another that now sees them—the cornerstone of resilient relationships.

Table 13.1 highlights progressive attempts toward identifying strengths representative of resilient living. From Wagnild and Young's (1990) themes of resilience, and Wolin and Wolin's (1993) challenge model of resilient strength categories, to the characteristics of strengths as proposed by Peterson and Seligman (2004), to the strength qualities as identified by Ward and Reuter (2011), a concerted effort has been made to provide a common vocabulary to describe and understand how human strengths provide protection against and preparation for future difficulties. Frank (1987) asserted that therapeutic interaction is successful only to the extent that it helps clients transform the meanings of their experiences. Being able to elicit and recognize strengths in others requires a vocabulary vastly different from the medicalized terminology of empiricism. Inviting others to consider how life struggles reflect their efforts of resilience is dependent on a language infused with possibilities, preferences, values, and strengths already present in managing their life circumstances.

TABLE 13.1 Development of Strength Understanding

Themes of Resilience, Wagnild & Young (1990)	Strength Categories, Wolin & Wolin (1993)	Strength Characteristics, Seligman (2008)	Strength Qualities, Ward & Reuter (2011)
• Equanimity (Life perspective)	• Insight (Reflective)	• Wisdom and knowledge (Use of knowledge)	• Creativity, curiosity, open-mindedness, learning, perspective
• Self-reliance (Self-efficacy)	• Independence (Internal locus)	• Courage (Exercise of will)	• Valor, persistence, integrity
• Existential aloneness (Uniqueness)	• Relationships (Loving well)	• Humanity and love (Befriending others)	• Honesty, responsibility, vitality
• Perseverance (Tenacity)	• Initiative (Drive)	• Justice (Civic responsibility)	• Caring, kindness, generosity
• Hardiness (Strength awareness)	• Creativity (Innovative)	• Temperance (Protect against Excess)	• Social intelligence, empathic
• Meaningfulness (Opportunities)	• Morality	• Transcendence (Connection to the larger universe)	• Loyalty, teamwork, fairness
	• (Integrity)		• Leadership, organizing, decisive
	• Humor (Playfulness)		• Forgiveness, humility, accepting
			• Prudence, cautious, disciplined
			• Appreciative, grateful, hopeful, faithful, optimistic, playful, spiritual

Influence of Culture

You have all seen the images: a person standing on a mountain top with arms outstretched to the heavens, an individual getting back up after falling down, or a single tree bending in the wind without breaking. They are images of perseverance, tenacity, and endurance, where individuals rise above the undercurrents of trauma, loss, and adverse life events. Understandably, resilience has been viewed as a "bouncing back" from adversity (Tugade & Frederickson, 2004) or recovery from negative incidents (Koshio et al., 2002; Sato, 2009). Studies have highlighted personality characteristics such as self-efficacy (Ryan & Deci, 2000), emotional control (Baumesister & Exline, 2000), and optimism (Peterson, 2000) as well as a variety of social protective factors (e.g., caregiving environment). Resilience, from this perspective, rests upon individual qualities and access to social resources to cope with stress and adversity. Although the identification and emphasis toward nurturing personal strengths in helping others withstand life adversities (rather than remediate psychosocial deficiencies) has been invaluable, it is also highly reflective of Western cultural themes, which highlight individualism, self-reliance, independence, autonomy, and self initiative.

In non-Western cultures, there is little separation between the self and others (Kondo, 1990; Rosenberger, 1992), especially as seen in the context of the community. Many non-Western cultures emphasize self-sacrifice rather than self-reliance or self-resilience (Iwasaki, 2005). Collectivistic cultures equate harmony with unity and life satisfaction (Kwan et al., 1997), and positive feelings are associated with interdependent relationships (Chang, 1988; Markus & Kitayama, 1999). It may be that a shared efficacy or communal mastery is far more indicative of resilience than individual grit. For example, a prospective study of 103 Native American women conducted by Hobfall et al. (2002) found that participants high in communal-mastery environments experienced less increase in depressive mood and anger when faced with high-stress circumstances than participants who were low in communal mastery. Having a positive cultural identity has also been shown to increase feelings of self-worth, self-efficacy, connectedness, and purpose (EchoHawk, 1997; Katz et al., 2006; White, 2000). It is possible that the research on resilience is so steeped in a Western-centric value system emphasizing individual qualities that it fails to incorporate culture and non-Western ideology (Ungar, 2013, 2017).

In collectivistic cultures, a strength perspective considers personal qualities in the context of others just as many of these cultures consider collective qualities imperative to personal well-being. This is especially true when addressing emotional distress. Studies suggested how positive and desirable emotional states are associated with a relational experience, such as friendliness, affiliation, calmness, smoothness, and connectedness (Kasai, 2009). Moreover, since the happiness and well-being of others matter so much in collectivist cultures, a strength language highlighting social connection and belonging, over individualism, is paramount. Table 13.2, developed by Ward and Sano (2015), highlights strengths from a culturally sensitive perspective emphasizing four relational categories: social relationships, collectivistic relationships, love relationships, and transcendent relationships. They contend that not only is resilience interdependent to relational quality but also that it only develops within the context of these relationships. Individual resilience is the outcome of relational support and represents an ever-increasing capacity for connection.

TABLE 13.2 Culturally Sensitive Strengths (Ward & Sano, 2015)

Strength categories	Strength qualities
Social relationships	Creativity, curiosity, open-mindedness, enthusiasm, generosity, courteousness, collaborative, perspective, loyalty
Collectivist relationships	Diligent, modest, humble, forgiving, discreet, merciful, restrained, disciplined, teamwork, adaptive
Love relationships	Caring, honest, lovable, original, playful, kind, intuitive, appreciative, good humored, empathic
Transcendent relationships	Grateful, appreciative, hopeful, believing in faith, optimistic, fair, brave, resolute

In collectivist cultures, resilience is manifested relationally (Leake & Black, 2005) and highlights how service, a commitment to one's community, reflects the interdependent bond between others and the importance of connection when seeking to live with resilience. Resilience is far more than an emphasis on self-reliance and autonomy and, instead, develops through shared experiences that help modulate dysregulating emotions and provide a container for holding silence without fear and connection over protection. The qualities of perseverance and tenacity, an endurance when finding meaning in even the most troubling life events, is not a solitary experience. Resilience is not a single tree bending in the wind or an individual arising alone in the darkness upon falling. It is other-reliant and interdependent: A tree stands tall when rooted within a grove, and all those that fall find support in the faith that others have in their strength to stand again. This, then, is the essence of resilience-centered counseling: a privileged experience where others are met on equal footing, viewed as capable, and held with respect to the inherent available strengths to arise, with others, and to lean into the wind.

Activity: Cultural Strengthening

With pen in hand, and referencing the charts above, reflect on the following questions:

- What aspects of your cultural experience might be influencing how you are holding your current struggle? What would be expected of you from a cultural perspective?
- Who held the cultural voice in your family? In what ways does this influence you today?
- Consider a moment when you were at your best (or closer to it). What strengths were you tapping into that seemed to give rise to your best self?
- How do you balance the values that are important to you today with cultural and family expectations?
- When you are closer to your best in reference to your gender, orientation, race, and so on, what might this say about what is important to you and what you might be learning about yourself?

Write down these reflections in a journal or discuss your reflections with a learning partner and consider how your reactions represent your cultural experiences as well as the quality of your relationships.

Remembering Our Better Self

Our view during times of intense stress can become so constricted that all we see, all we know, is how our stress, anxiety, or depression demands our attention. We are what we attune to, and if all we see is the worry of living, that is how we will live. Burns (1989), a cognitive theorist, argued that when governed by strong emotions, the mind becomes a filter, letting into awareness only those thoughts that reinforce that mood. In other words, the more someone reexperiences the negative moods associated with the problems presented in counseling, the more unlikely change will appear. Although exceptions are occurring all the time, people rarely stop to question this cycle or explore those times when problems had less influence on themselves and their lives. If they did, they are often dismissed as flukes, accidents, or trivial events.

When I was younger, I (Colin) went in to renew my driver's license, which required a brief vision test. This was accomplished by looking into a large box with images displayed on the screen. When told that I had failed the test, I immediately thought the box was malfunctioning and asked for a second screening. Some weeks later, I departed the optometrist office wearing my new prescription glasses and began the walk home. I had taken this route many times during my time in the city but was immediately struck by how new it all was. I saw, for the first time, the flowers in the baskets hanging from the streetlights. Store signs, traffic signals, and the faces of people that I passed all had a clarity unnoticed just a day before. Clearly, it was not the world around me that changed but how I perceived it: as if I was seeing it for the first time. Assisting others remember past competence, confidence, acceptance, and courage (positive emotions) can broaden one's gaze beyond the immediate and help anchor the preferred into something known but not seen.

Not only does this type of remembering help activate the PNS and open up access to our executive cognitive functions but the experience itself provides a "scaffold" from the known and familiar to the unknown and unfamiliar. Scaffolding is at the heart of a resilience-centered approach to counseling where a "stretch" from the immediate experience to past moments of personal, social, and cultural competence are made. In poetic terms, it is a mutual journey into the uncertainty of the "great unknown" while also setting benchmarks by remembering the certainty of the known. By recalling those periods of our life when we felt closer to our better self, we can, as Walter and Peller (1992) wrote, reveal seeds for future solutions. When these actions are anchored, in part, with memories associated with feelings of self-efficacy, confidence for change increases.

The questions below are an invitation to one's "best self" in resistance to anxious and worrisome thoughts. They can promote a mindset that empowers one to be in greater service to a set of personal strengths and values rather than in reaction to stress-producing situations or interactions. In many ways we become what we can predict. To inoculate oneself against the neurobiological reaction to high levels of anxiety and fear is to bring increased access to executive brain function: an intentional response in service to a preferred mindset rather than in reaction to a protective stress response (flight, fight, and freeze). With a partner (if possible; otherwise, this can be completed with pen in hand), consider a recent moment when you were closer to your better self and have a shared conversation to the questions below. Seek to do so without interpretation, only remembering those times that, although not perfect, represented more of who you seek to be more often. Paint a picture in your mind's eye upon completion and note any physical or emotional sensations.

- What was different about you in that moment than from other life moments?
- What feelings were more alive in you?
- What strengths might you have been tapping into that seemed to give rise to your better self?
- What values were you holding close? What seemed at the forefront of your mind?
- What was alive in you that others might have witnessed during this moment in time? What did they receive from you and you from them?

Strengthening Requires Sacrifice

Empirical models often seek to replace the known (e.g., symptoms of worry, anxiety, and depression) with thoughts and actions that are unknown and foreign. A client's unwillingness to step into the deep abyss of fear and uncertainty to the untried and unknown is often interpreted as resistance by well-meaning clinicians. It highlights a binary view where health is represented by the absence of the problem or symptoms and is paramount to asking people with a fear of water to swim by jumping into the deep end of the pool. Hesitancy and fear would be natural reactions when invited to try something both new and dangerous: a danger often imperceptible from those privileged with the skills and confidence for swimming. Resilience-centered clinicians consider not just the desired outcomes as expressed by clients but also the experience to what it might take, and the sacrifice required, in order to begin.

Consider someone in your life (e.g., client, colleague, friend, yourself) that is in the midst of a struggle. Imagine their struggle as experienced by them and reflect on the questions below:

- What are they sacrificing that keeps the struggle alive?
- What is the struggle robbing them of?
- What might the absence of the struggle mean for them, both in terms of personal freedoms and profound loss?

We all have untold stories of resilience where we sacrifice the possible for something else: joy for security, hope for resignation, love for loneliness, and support for isolation. Suffering is self-protective and, therefore, representative of resilient efforts. It is part of an ever-present life force to meet our essential needs for safety, affiliation, competence, and relational meaning. By focusing on the struggle against daily problems rather than just the problem and/or solution itself, the dynamic qualities of personal resilience can be explored. Appreciating the strengths and dedicated commitments that people bring to bear on life challenges is to appreciate the complexity of living. By attuning to how clients experience their story rather than focusing on the story itself, efforts of resilience and the strengths reflective therein emerge. By acknowledging these reflective truths, to see the struggle from a perspective of strength rather than of defeat, is to bring life back into the therapeutic conversation and within the client. They are not the problem; the problem is the problem (White & Epston, 1990).

Two Wolves

A Cherokee elder speaks to his grandson about life. "A battle rages inside me," he says. "It is dangerous, and it is between two wolves. One is evil. He is anger, envy, sorrow, regret, arrogance, self-pity, guilt, resentment, lies, superiority, and ego." He continued, "The other is good. He is joy, peace, love, hope, serenity, humility, kindness, empathy, generosity, truth, and faith. The same fight goes on inside of you and inside of everyone else as well." The grandson pondered his words and asked, "Which wolf will win?"

The old Cherokee smiled and replied, "If you feed them right, they both win." The story goes on:

You see, if I only feed the white wolf, the black wolf will hide in the dark waiting for me to falter so that it can pounce and get the attention he craves. He will always be angry and will always be fighting the white wolf. But if I acknowledge him, both he and the white wolf can be satisfied, and we all win.

For the black wolf has qualities that I need and that the white wolf lacks: tenacity, courage, fearlessness, strength of will, and resourcefulness. The white wolf instead provides compassion, caring, heart, and the ability to value the needs of others over my own.

You see, the two wolves need each other. Feeding only one and starving the other will eventually make both uncontrollable. Caring for both allows them both to serve you so that you can do something greater, something good with your time on earth. Feed them both and you will quiet their internal struggle for your attention, and, when there is no battle inside, you can then hear the voices of deeper knowledge that will guide you in choosing the right path in every circumstance.

Highlighting the personal, relational, and cultural strengths inherent in every life struggle is to (a) separate who the person is from what is happening to them and (b) provide an opportunity to access additional strengths. The clinical direction for both the counselor and client is a mutual discovery of increasing the availability of strengths rather than the absence of deficits. For example, caution and restraint can be useful, especially during times of intense emotional distress; however, the dichotomy of these strengths can be indecision and missed opportunities when taking responsibility for life choices. Compassion toward the welfare of others can lead to resenting the sacrifice of personal needs.

Although this therapeutic gaze can have a profound influence on the shift from "feeling better" to "feeling stronger," it is often unfamiliar for both therapists and their clients. It is far easier to articulate what is lacking than what is abundant. The expression of what is "going wrong" often overshadows that which is "going right," and the urge to focus on the experience of others distracts from a focus inward. An example of this is often illustrated in my role as a counseling supervisor. In recounting a counseling session, a supervisee will often, in detail, express all that should have been done or said as well as the many opportunities missed to intervene differently with their clientele. The temptation to perceive efforts that fall short of our expectations as statements of personal failure is available to all of us. For supervisees, this can diminish the inherent complexities associated with their professional growth and thwart the necessary risk-taking actions needed for increasing their professional confidence. As you might have guessed, since you have made it this far in the text, we suggest that you respond not by delving into their shortcomings but by better understanding the "rest of the story" to the session: What are you learning about yourself in working with this client that appears to be making a difference in your relationship? The discovery of inherent personal qualities that make a difference, considering "something different" is the essence of strengthening and essential in providing the foundation for future change.

Below are reflective prompts to attune to and elicit strength qualities in others. They are not interventions but are designed to shift the gaze of change away from pathology and a binary perspective of healing and toward the inherent nature of self-healing and worth. Assisting clients and families with understanding their struggles through a context of strengths and possibilities rather than personal deficits and problems instills hope for change. With a learning partner (or in reflection with a client), have a shared conversation around acknowledging the presence of resilient qualities, the dichotomous nature of strengths and wisdom, and an exploration to a more resilient and strength-centered mindset. Please use the strength tables above to assist in your discussion and do so without judgment or reassurance. Perceived strengths are reflective of the storyteller as they tell their stories, not the listener.

- *Acknowledgment*: What would you (or others) say are the qualities that keep you going during difficult times? How do they keep your head above water? What is your theory about how they developed? Who has had the most influence on their development, and in what ways?

- *Dichotomies*: Strengths are representative of our resilient efforts but can also get the best of us at times. How might this be true for you? What other strengths might you wish to tap into at times? What might you need to release in order to hold these new strengths closer? Who would support your decision to broaden your repertoire of interpersonal strengths?

- *Wisdoms*: How would you summarize the wisdom you hope to continue to take from your current struggle/life events? What do these wisdoms say about your deepest values?

- *Mindset*: Reflect on your preferred strengths above. Imagine being more in service to these strengths rather than in reaction to situations or others. While doing so, attune to your body and notice the sensation of where these preferred strengths reside.

Even the smallest recognition of our better self is revitalizing—and an essential building block for living, growth, and choice. Rather than seeking the absence of the struggle or the reduction of suffering, it is a therapeutic intent to elicit personal qualities often hidden by misery, protective strategies, and the failure to achieve goals set by others.

Top Takeaways

1. Strengths are not qualities that we provide others, as this would reflect more about the counselor's need to comfort than the client's need to be comforted. Rather, they are emergent truths reflected in our struggle to heal, overcome, and find meaning.

2. Being able to elicit and recognize strengths in others requires a vocabulary vastly different from the medicalized terminology of empiricism. Inviting others to consider how life struggles

reflect their efforts of resilience is dependent on a language infused with possibilities, preferences, values, and strengths already present in managing their life circumstances.

3. In collectivistic cultures, a strength perspective considers personal qualities in the context of others just as many of these cultures consider collective qualities imperative to personal well-being.

4. Although exceptions are occurring all the time, people rarely stop to question this cycle or explore those times when problems had less influence on themselves and their lives. If they did, they are often dismissed as flukes, accidents, or trivial events.

5. Hesitancy and fear would be natural reactions when invited to try something both new and dangerous: a danger often imperceptible from those privileged with confidence. Resilience-centered clinicians consider not just the desired outcomes as expressed by clients but also the experience to what it might take and the sacrifice required in order to begin.

An Integrative Guide for Resilience-Centered Counseling

The secret to getting ahead is to get started.
—*Mark Twain*

This is a guide to an integrated approach to resilience-centered counseling. It is not a manual and is not to be used as an assessment. The questions are prompts to intentionally shift a shared conversation toward a holding of client struggles, a remembering of their better selves, and an opening of space for increased personal, social, and cultural agency in their lives. Each feature requires counselors to enter the therapeutic encounter with wonder, acceptance, and unfaltering belief in the restorative capacity of people to marshal the needed resources for transforming stress and trauma into units of meaning that serve to sustain them. This also includes a social justice stance that freely shares power and, as a witness to the growth of others, facilitates a broadening to the choices and resources available to people as they take back their lives from oppression and suffering. These features are fluid at the disposal of the counselor: At any time with clients, they may hold space, engage remembering, highlight resilience, and open space so that life dissonance is addressed and transformed into both something known and something about to be known.

RCC features	Prompts
Holding space	• **Client experience:** What impact has this problem/struggle had on you and your relationships? What does it reveal to you that you can believe about yourself?
	• **Client sacrifice:** What has the problem/struggle robbed you of? What might the absence of the struggle mean for you, both in terms of personal freedoms and profound loss?
	• **Client context:** What has influenced this belief (e.g., eco-map of family, culture, socio/political culture)? Who might be pleased that you came to counseling, and how come?
	• **Client preference:** What do you imagine might be different about you if took back even a small bit of your life from this issue/struggle/problem? What might you need to let go of or come to terms with to make this possible?
	• **Client agency:** How much of your life does it control? Are you ok with this? What is that like to say out loud?

RCC features	Prompts
Remembering	**Vitality (zest):** Recall a moment of recent pleasure or vitality when you felt the energy of being closer to your better self. • What feelings were more alive with you? • What seemed more open to you? • What was alive in you that others might have witnessed during this moment? What did they receive from you and you from them? **Better self (values):** Imagine what you would like to remember about yourself: • What strengths will you apply (e.g., openness, optimism, honesty) that will be more in service to your personal values (e.g., kindness, compassion, contribution)? • What compassion for yourself would help to keep your anxious thoughts at bay? What do you notice (ideas, feelings, sensations) as irritation and worry have less of hold on you? What wisdom does this carry for you? • (Option for relationships): How can you remember that the best way to reduce interpersonal conflict is to hold space for multiple perspectives rather than only your own, which can lead to blame and resentment? • What do you notice in what you are experiencing in this moment? **Exceptions (revisions):** Given the impact this struggle/problem has on you, tell me about times when it has less influence over you: • What is different about you when are a bit more able to keep your head above water? What is your guess on how you are able to do that at those times? • What is different about those times when things are bit more on track? What is your guess about how you are able to keep the problem at bay a bit better? • When the problem is less present, what are you thinking about instead? What ideas and activities seem more available? • What is your guess about what others might notice in you when the problem is less present?
Strengthening (See strength qualities)	• **Acknowledgment:** What would you (or others) say are the qualities that keep you going during difficult times? How do they help you keep your head above water? What is your theory about how they developed? Who has had the most influence on their development, and in what ways? • **Dichotomies:** Strengths are representative of our resilient efforts but can also get the best of us at times. How might this be true for you? What other strengths might you wish to tap into at these times? What might you need to release or modify in order to hold these new strengths closer? Who else might support your decision to broaden your repertoire of interpersonal strengths? • **Wisdoms:** How would you summarize the wisdom you hope to continue to take from your current struggle/life events? What do these wisdoms suggest about your deepest values? • **Mindset:** Reflect on your preferred strengths above. Imagine being more in service to these strengths rather than in reaction to situations or others. While doing so, attune to your body and notice the sensation of where these preferred strengths reside.

(Continued)

RCC features	Prompts
Cultural strengths	• What aspects of your cultural experience might be influencing how you are holding your current struggle? What would be expected of you from a cultural perspective?
	• Who held the cultural voice in your family? In what ways does this influence you today?
	• Consider a moment when you were at your best (or closer to it). What strengths were you tapping into that seemed to give rise to your best self?
	• When you are closer to your best in reference to your gender, orientation, race, and so on, what might this say about what is important to you, and what you might be learning about yourself?
Resilient efforts	**Connection:** What would others say are the qualities that keep you going during these difficult times? Who has influenced the development of these qualities/ strengths, and in what ways?
	Culture: How do you balance the values that are important to you with cultural and family expectations? What other beliefs and traditions do you share? What values do you embody that are in disagreement with your local and larger culture? How does that show up? Do you want to change your values or influence the local or larger culture? How might that work begin?
	Community: What values would you like to be in greater service to? Beyond yourself, what you like to be giving to more, and in what ways? What would this mean to you if these actions were more present in your life?
	Capacity: How have you managed to keep your head above water in the face of this struggle? What has sustained you … even just a bit? What would you like to be more available to yourself, and you with others?
Opening space	**Wisdoms:**
	• What wisdoms do you imagine might be on the other side of this struggle?
	• What might these wisdoms say about your deepest values?
	Envisioning: Imagine a time down the road when the two of us meet again and, during the time between now and then, you had figured some things out for yourself.
	• What might you say you had come to peace with?
	• What feels more possible in your life and in yourself?
	• What is something you know you can bear that at some point in your life was considered unbearable?
	• What might you need to remind yourself of when life again throws you a curve ball?
	Immediacy: Take a moment and briefly scan for sensations you are noticing in yourself—and do this without judgment (as much as you can).
	• What images or thoughts are you aware of in this moment as we consider the better parts of yourself and paths forward from here?
	• What parts of yourself are more accessible that may wish to take with you today— to notice as the week unfolds?

Conclusion

Purpose of This Book

The purpose of this book was to open you up as a therapist to a set of ideas and ways of being with people that are helpful and other centered. As we have pointed out repeatedly, many aspects of our mental health systems, theories, models, and interventions either end up not being helpful or, worse, iatrogenic, thus violating the first order of our collective ethics codes: First, do no harm. This does not say it is okay to do unintended harm, though that may be inevitable. This does not say it is okay to have good intentions and harm, though that will likely happen in your careers. This does not say as long as you engage in evidence-based practices in what you do with clients, doing harm is excusable. Again, what it says is *first do no harm*!

Most mental health training programs for counselors, marriage and family therapists, and psychologists will spend a great deal of time and energy training you to detect and treat mental disorders. We have collectively been through all that training, and we still have serious questions about what exactly we are training people to actually do for those who seek shelter in counseling from the storms of life. We see many of the shelters that we were trained to provide as being built out of deficits, problems, trauma explorations, paradoxes, treatment plans, intervention models, philosophies, and epistemologies. In our training we confer much of client change on what we do with others. We do not see much about shelters that work consistently: the shelters that clients construct. Coming to understand that process allows us the opportunity to provide a safe environment and a relationship for construction to thrive. People seek us out to find the means to become who they are and would prefer to be.

When you were a child visiting a friend's house for the first time and that friend showed you around, did you know where all the stuff you would play with was stored? How about the food for snacks? If you were invited back, eventually you might discover the secret places, if you were trusted. You might even discover the rules of the house and the family culture. If you became best friends, you would discover and eventually share your secrets, fantasies, dreams, aspirations, and desires. If you were lucky enough to become long-term friends, you would be privileged to watch how all that grows, changes, and/or stays the same. It truly is a privileged place to be a best friend, even one of many. Do you diagnose your best friend? Do you employ a model where only you have the expertise in how it works in interacting with your best friend? We think not. You trust and enjoy each other, learn from each other, and experience the world together. Although a counseling relationship is not friendship, the dynamics that shed light on those aspects of a relationship promoting well-being and growth are similar.

It was once said (we do not exactly know by who) that seeing a counselor or therapist is like renting a good parent. Often, when clinicians rely solely on models, treatment plans, interventions, and attempting to be that rented good parent, the client's agenda can get lost or watered down in favor of the therapist's agenda. We have concluded that the best way to stay focused on the client agenda is to stay focused on the client: the whole client. Becoming aware of the client as a fully functioning system of attributes and resiliencies will assist in rounding out a view of clients enabling you to celebrate their accomplishments, histories, values, desires, and dreams. Model or theory driven therapy has the potential to overemphasize the role of therapists on the premise that (a) theories can accurately describe the human condition and (b) understanding client pathology is a requirement for effective treatment planning. People in context are far more complicated than what can be observed and described by professional assumptions, and the absence of symptoms, suffering, or problems has little to do with what most people seek from counseling professionals: change.

When training counselors and psychologists to diagnose people, the diagnosis can take center stage, leaving the client in the orchestra pit, almost like a passive observer. It can quickly garner the lion's share of our attention as therapists. It is only natural to pay attention to what is wrong. I (Bill) had a classmate who was lucky enough to be close personal friends with the famous psychologist Albert Ellis. My classmate informed me a number of years ago that he was invited to attend Dr. Ellis's centennial birthday celebration. My friend asked me if I had any questions for the great Dr. Ellis. I arrogantly asked him to ask why it was we remember bad things more readily than good things. He obliged me, and when he gained a private audience with Dr. Ellis, he reported that he asked Dr. Ellis my question. Dr. Ellis did not hesitate to answer. He flatly stated, "Tell your classmate he is an idiot! If we didn't do it that way, we would all be dead!" (G. Neiders, personal communication, September 2006). We are attracted to problems and even horrific events like moths to a flame. It can be a trance-like experience that we return to again and again. This seems to be a hard-wired survival reaction we all share. Thus, learning taxonomies of human problems and behaviors comes to us naturally. It has served our evolutionary process and improved our abilities to survive. That is until it becomes a problem in and of itself. Suggesting that we as clinicians refrain from diagnosing problems would be a fool's errand. It is listening to people without being overly distracted by it that we are advocating.

At first glance, it may seem impossible to look past the wreckage that accompanies many clients. Well, it is impossible! We do not think ignoring the wreckage is the right thing to do. We must acknowledge and validate our client's experience without allowing the experience to become our idea of who the client is. People are far more than their histories or what has happened to them. Their problems do not illustrate deficiencies or weakness but resilient efforts in pursuit of something preferred in the face of something that is not. By focusing on the inherent worth and capacity of clients, restoration, rather than treatment, is possible. This is the cornerstone of ethical and effective clinical practice: emphasizing a positive, wholistic approach to people and their capabilities as opposed to a preoccupied view of their deficits.

Openness

In systems theory our predecessors have discovered that closed systems tend to get rigid and in time may collapse on themselves or implode, falling into dysfunction, while open systems allow for new information to enter, be processed, and used for the benefit of that system. This enhanced capability of open systems creates a climate and context for growth, adaptability, and flexibility—in other words, *resilience*! When we open ourselves to possibilities, we open our clients to possibilities. When we wonder aloud about what might come next or wonder at our client's future wondering, we reify possibilities. Often, people come to us because they are stuck in the trance of the problem (B. Bertolino, personal communication, 2010) or they seem to be out of ideas and appear stuck in the cycle of doing the same thing over and over (e.g., trauma reenactments). As we have pointed out, the reenactment process is resilience that simply needs to be recalibrated by the client. By allowing the client to question and seek additional ideas or ways of doing things, a reenactment can shift from a repetitive problem pattern to one that paves the way for the posttraumatic growth they are seeking and have accomplished with other situations in the past.

By becoming open to client abilities as opposed to what may become an exclusive focus on their disabilities, we find a treasure trove of untapped resources, ideas, theories, approaches, and solutions to problems right there in the client! There is little chance of rejection of those ideas or what some might call "resistance," as the source of the ideas and approaches come from the client. By being open to what the client already brings to the change process, we are modeling how clients can be open to themselves and to their indigenous inherent knowledge with a renewed confidence and efficacy to act on their own behalf. Our goal as therapists is to recognize the client capacities and assist them in making them available to themselves on an ongoing basis.

Reflective Practice

By recognizing the client as a whole system, we must, at the same time, recognize ourselves as a whole system interacting with the various client systems. This view allows us to contextualize the client as an operating system influenced on multiple levels in multiple ways. It also allows us the same opportunity to view ourselves as people, as counselors/therapists/consultants/participants in the world and in the lives of our clients. We must tend to our own systems and become clear about what belongs to us, what we share, and what we do not share. This is essentially reflective practice: a cyclical process where counselors consider their affective, cognitive, and behavioral experiences to inform their assumptions and work with others (Goodyear, 2005; Schon, 1987). Reflectivity will enhance both your procedural knowledge of the therapy process as well as gauging your experience while experiencing your clients. It is essentially a way to work from the inside out, examining how you influence (or overinfluence) your work with clients. These reflective questions might include:

- What is it like to sit in the room with this client? How would you describe your experience with this client? With their hurt or trauma?

- How is this similar to past conflicts or interactions? What have you learned about yourself? What might still need to be resolved?

- In what ways might your own experience be informing you of your client's experience? How might the pull of countertransference be hampering your work with them?

- What do you wish for yourself as you move forward with this client? What do you hope to learn from them? How might you support this learning? Would answers to these questions be good issues to bring to supervision or consultation?

There is an old folk tale of a student who, in seeking wisdom from a master, was asked if they would care for tea. As the master poured, the tea began to spill over the brim of the cup and onto the lap of student. The student cried out, "The cup is full!" with the master quickly replying, "As are you." Reflective practice will require you to suspend all that you know and "empty your cup" so that you might approach yourself and others with an openness, mitigating bias or judgment and enhancing curiosity. It can evoke a cognitive complexity, or the ability to integrate and make use of multiple perspectives (multiplicity), that is linked to greater empathy and less prejudice and greater focus on the counseling process rather than on the counselor (Ober, 2009). Additional professional disposition, as noted by Gardner et al. (2016), that also appear consistent with advanced counseling competence include:

Conscientiousness	Accepting responsibility, dependable, self-discipline
Self-awareness	Knowledge and impact of one's traits, emotions, behaviors on others
Interpersonal skills	Demonstrating warmth and energy in interpersonal relationships
Emotional stability	Ability to control negative emotions and adopt a positive perspective
Moral reasoning	Behavior reflecting honesty, reliability, and truthful dealings with others
Openness	Tolerance for ambiguity, lifestyles of others, and open to new learning
Cultural sensitivity	Sensitivity to multiple factors that make up an individual's identity and awareness of their own beliefs on others

Doing your own work with yourself on an ongoing basis is essential for you to become and develop those dispositions illustrative of effective counselors. Being clear about what difficulties you have or are experiencing in your work with others not only heralds increased openness, reflectivity, and conceptual complexity but is also in service to our mandate of doing no harm. We therefore challenge each of you to (a) journal and engage in reflective professional practice, (b) maintain regular supervision and consultation, (c) go to therapy, (d) stay in therapy, (e) explore what your capabilities and abilities are and what they may not be, and (f) resolve to continue doing that work for you and those you will be privileged to serve in the days ahead.

Models and Applications: How Much Is Enough?

Over the decades there has been a gradual movement away from theory-driven approaches to counseling. From eclecticism (toolbox of techniques), assimilative integration (parent theory with techniques from other approaches), and common factors (efficiency factors across theories), developing a personalized counseling theory organized around a set of principles essential to human change and renewal has been growing (Jones-Smith, 2020). This book, and the chapters therein, illustrate an integrative theoretical context for effective therapy grounded in the essential ideas of self-healing and interdependency to provide a resilient framework, centered on the client expertise, to assist in their suffering and become, for lack of a better word, stronger. It is not a book of techniques or interventions that can risk stripping away the power of those we are seeking to counsel. This book was written to empower clinicians to adopt a gaze that invites us to focus and include the best of clients as a topic equal and in time carrying greater weight in the conversation between clients and counselors.

We are often asked by students and clinicians alike: what models should we use? Which ones are best? How many should we have in our toolboxes? The Ericksonian psychologist Stephen Gilligan provides us with some guidance for this question. If we are to view the client's story as a metaphor and the over 500 different psychotherapy models as metaphors, then our task as therapists is simply to match the client's metaphor with the model metaphor that best fits the client's situation (Gilligan & Price, 1993). So, the answer to the question of what models and how many is really subjective. It is probably a good idea to know at least a couple of psychotherapy models for each class of such models. One way to slice this up is to assess the types of clients you are seeing or wish to do work within your practice.

Norcross (2020) informs us that people arrive in therapy at various stages in their willingness to change: precontemplative, contemplative, action, and maintenance. His work informs us that different models may be better suited for use at various stages of change. One issue stands out and that is that relational models work well at any stage, others are more effective at different stages, and some are ineffective at various stages and may be a mismatch. Relationship dynamics (e.g., empathy, positive regard, collaboration), regardless of theoretical orientation or approach, is the primary predictor of successful counseling outcomes (Norcross & Lambert, 2019). Furthermore, assisting clients with utilizing their strengths and available resources affects the overall outcome of counseling (Cuijpers et al., 2021). It becomes less about what happens in counseling and more about how counseling sessions inform clients about themselves. As noted by Bohort and Tallman (2010), "The emphasis should be more on helping clients use their own resources to change rather than applying standardized treatment packages" (pp. 99–100).

We are suggesting that the client is aware of where they are and where they want to be on some level, and it is our task to first discover those positions the client has assumed and attempt to understand what is being expressed and what the person is attempting to resolve. Therefore, knowledge of many different types of models would be advantageous and increase the likelihood of matching metaphors. By focusing on the strengths and inherent capabilities of people to recover from life's challenges, and to do so with unwavering acceptance and curiosity, is to embody the best in counseling practice and provides clients with the greatest opportunity for positive outcomes.

Helping clients unveil their inherent resilient capacities requires counselors to do the same. It is impossible to fully use a tool with others that is unfamiliar to oneself. Practicing resilience-centered counseling requires counselors to do the work in acknowledging their strengths and values as they examine the very contexts, cultural influences, and attributes that they seek to explore with others. It is a commitment by clinicians to write (and rewrite) their own narrative of who they are, what they need to come to terms with, and who they hope to become. As obvious as it may sound, counselors are people too. The struggles of our clients are struggles we are familiar with. By acknowledging rather than bracketing common stories of the human experience, counselors can remove their own voice, vision, and expectations from the lived experiences of others and in turn, encourage them to be free to choose their own journey. This is not only the essence of resilience-centered counseling, but of a liberative therapeutic stance that accentuates the voice of clients as they make meaning of their lives and within their relationships. How is it that many counselor, social worker, and psychologist training programs continue to spend an inordinate amount of time on teaching counseling techniques rather than focusing on the tool available to all counseling professionals—themselves?

The degree to which we have some understanding of who we are and how we came to be that person appears to be the degree to which we can discern what belongs to us and what belongs to our client; what is truly different and what is similar; and how to keep them separate so that we can operate with and in support of our clients as opposed to being enmeshed with them and caught in the trance of their problems. The first and most importat task in any therapy encounter is to advocate for and provide a safe space. This safe space is a temporary shelter from the storms of life, where a person can catch their breath and be still long enough to see past the crisis of the moment and into their strengths and capabilities so that they can liberate themselves from whatever has or is oppressing their agency and become who they aspire to be.

The Death of the Expert—Except in a Crisis

We have not advocated for the abandonment of expertise, only the expert. Expertise is a valuable asset in any profession and especially so in this one. Being in the role of expert is often a barrier to access who our clients are, what they value, and where they want to go. We are advocating for an egalitarian approach, as we find in feminist and postmodern approaches. It is a difficult task to resign as the expert when we have expertise. It seems paradoxical to assert that for your expertise to be effective with the most people that you need to actively resign as the expert and assume a "not-knowing mind" with each client encounter. Impossible? Perhaps—and necessary for a true empathic relationship and connection to consistently arise. These connections will be initially fragile and tentative, and they must be persistently attended to in order to flourish and pave the way for people to grow and thrive. It may seem paradoxical that we are suggesting that we need to resign as experts while constantly acquiring more and more expertise. That is exactly what we are advocating for throughout this book, and it is our hope each of you makes a commitment to this preposterous suggestion as a lifelong work. Learning and our capacity to learn is perhaps the most essential resiliency of all. It is through learning that we gain confidence and a sense of our own efficacy.

It is also learning that continually provides opportunities for an openness to new ideas and ways of experiencing our clients in much the same way we are asking clients to explore themselves and the world around them. An openness to learning is also an openness to persistently seek the rest of the person, the unique and various systems in which each of us is embedded, along with the miraculous capacity to internalize what we need to survive and thrive. Waters and Asbil (2013) envision this through the lens of cultural humility, where counselors (a) commit to continuous self-evaluation and critique, (b) seek to fix imbalances of power, and (c) aspire to develop partnerships that advocate for others. To stand with others in this way is to collaboratively discover the complexity of identities, cultures, intersections, and narrative structures that oppress. This is the essence of resilience-centered counseling and is much more difficult.

There is one exception to the resignation as an expert and that is when exigent circumstances arise, as in assisting a suicidal or homicidal client. When there is serious risk to self or others, our hats need to change from empathic therapist to crisis responder and being a manager with expertise may become essential. Keep in mind that often the measures and actions we take when in this role may sacrifice the therapy relationship to save a life. Though it may be painful, it is worth the cost in those instances.

Top Challenges

Challenge 1: Do your own work first. Nobody expects you to be perfectly mentally healthy. We do expect you to become aware of your own issues, problems, strengths, and resiliencies. In other words, heal thyself (with a good therapist).

Challenge 2: Know your enemy! Our enemy is not the *DSM-V* but what people often do with it. The well-intentioned iatrogenic effects that often result from such far-removed, professional descriptions of problems must be challenged when they occur. Knowing these systems will allow you the vision to see when preoccupation with the problem and diffuse descriptions (labels) at the expense of strengths and resiliencies so that you may act on behalf of what is working, and not just in opposition to what is a problem.

Challenge 3: Listen for what is right, not just that what is wrong. People are burdened by what feels wrong in their lives and in themselves. Symptoms are personalized as reflections of their failings and struggles as evidence of their weakness. They seek counseling to seek relief, with the hopes that what is wrong can be fixed. Refrain from a helping relationship were one who perceives themselves as broken seeks another who agrees and prescribes treatment. It will rob you of working from a perspective of strengths, where symptoms may be less about what is wrong and more about what has been working. Together, you can discover what is right.

Challenge 4: Seek a therapeutic gaze that acknowledges people as far more than the symptoms they describe and far more capable of change than what might seem possible. Too often, the inherent strengths of others go unrecognized, unnamed, and unused between clients and counselors. The best in all of us can be shrouded by the difficulty of the next step and the struggle toward a better life. Shine a light on the strengths, values, and qualities of yourself and those you seek to serve: These are often forgotten by time and undernourished by fate. If you work together with your clients, suffering can be transformed into strengths, despair into hope, and loneliness into a greater sense of connection.

Challenge 5: Remember the 4 Cs of resilience. *Connect* with others by noting the experience of their story rather than the story itself. Accentuate *cultural* identity and reflections of belonging. Observe how people *connect* what they hope to receive and give to one another. Finally, believe in the *capacity* of your clients so that they may be in greater service to their deepest ideals as well as to the communities in which they live.

Challenge 6: Dimensionalize and contextualize people. Develop a view of everyone you encounter as imbedded in a series of concentric systems that all conspire to encourage the behaviors they engage in (your behaviors too!). Understand that everyone is doing the best that they can in that moment.

Challenge 7: Become a forever learner! Keep adding to your library of information. Go to seminars of interest. Affiliate with great counselors and therapists (you will meet many of them at training seminars). *Question everything* and wait patiently for the answers.

Challenge 8: Read a novel now and then, okay?! Go to or rent a movie, something mindless or funny (Bill recommends *Airplane*). Take long walks on sunny days and breath in deep and often. Go on a long drive in the country, find a stream or a spot with a view, and just sit there and take it in. If you do not have a hobby, something you love to do just for the sake of doing it, then explore things until something grabs you. Give it a try!

Warmly,
Colin, Bill, and Katherine

References

Adler, A. (1927). The feeling of inferiority and the striving for recognition. *Proceedings of the Royal Society of Medicine, 20*(2), 1881–1886.

Adler, A. (1937). Psychiatric aspects regarding individual and social disorganization. *American Journal of Sociology, 42*(6).

Adler, A. (1964). *Problems of neurosis.* Harper Torchbooks.

The American Heritage dictionary of the English language. (2009). Houghton Mifflin.

American Psychiatric Association. (1987). *Diagnostic and statistical manual of mental disorders* (3rd rev. ed.).

Anderson, H., & Goolishian, H. (1992). The client is the expert: A not-knowing approach to therapy. In S. McNamee & K. J. Gergen (Eds.), *Therapy as social construction* (pp. 25–39). Sage Publications, Inc.

Anzaldúa, G. (1987). *Borderlands/La Frontera: The new mestiza.* Aunt Lute Books.

Baker, K. (2018). *Imagining a world.* Thorton Press.

Ballou, M., Hill, M., & West, C. (2008). *Feminist therapy theory and practice: A contemporary perspective.* Springer Publishing Company.

Ballou, M., Matsumoto, A., & Wagner, M. (2002). Toward a feminist ecological theory of human nature: Theory building in response to real-world dynamics. In M. Ballou & L. S. Brown (Eds.), *Rethinking mental health and disorder: Feminist perspectives* (pp. 99–141). Guilford Press.

Beck, A. T., Rush, A., Shaw, B., & Emery, G. (1979). *Cognitive therapy of depression.* The Guilford Press.

Bell, L. G., Dendo, H., Nakata, Y., Bell, D. C., Munakata, T., & Nakarmura, S. (2004). The experience of family in Japan and the United States: Working with the constraints inherent in the cross-cultural research. *Journal of Comparative Family Studies, 35*(3), 351–373.

Bertalanffy, L. (1968). *Organismic psychology and systems theory.* Clark University Press.

Bertolino, B., & O'Hanlon, B. (2002). *Collaborative competency-based counseling and therapy.* Allyn and Bacon.

Bohart, A. C., & Tallman, K. (2010). Clients: The neglected common factor in psychotherapy. In B. L. Duncan, S. D. Miller, B. E. Wampold, & M. A. Hubble (Eds.), *The heart and soul of change: Delivering what works in therapy* (pp. 83–111). American Psychological Association.

Bolles, R. C. (1991). *The hedonics of taste.* Lawrence Erlbaum Associates.

Bonanno, G. A. (2004). Loss, trauma, and human resilience: Have we underestimated the human capacity to thrive after extremely aversive events? *American Psychologist, 59*(1), 20–28.

Bonhoeffer, D. (1940). *Conspiracy and imprisonment.* Fortress Press.

Boscolo, L., Cecchin, G., Hoffman, L., & Penn, P. (1987). *Milan systemic family therapy: Conversations in theory and practice.* Basic Books.

Bowen, M. (1978). *Family therapy in clinical practice.* Jason Aronson.

Bowlby, J. (1977). The making and breaking of affectional bonds: I. Aetiology and psychopathology in the light of attachment theory. *The British Journal of Psychiatry, 130*(3), 201–210.

Brack, C. J., Brack, G., & Zucker, A. (1995). How chaos and complexity theory can help counselors to be more effective. *Counseling and Values, 39*(3), 200–208.

Breur, J., & Freud, S. (1950). *Studies in hysteria.* Beacon Press. (Original work published 1937)

Bronfenbrenner, U. (2005). Ecological systems theory. In U. Bronfenbrenner (Ed.), *Making human beings human: Bioecological perspectives on human development* (pp. 106–173). Sage Publications.

Brough, P. (2004). Comparing the influence of traumatic and organizational stressors on the psychological health of police, fire, and ambulance officers. *International Journal of Stress Management, 11*(3), 227–244.

Bruner, J. (1960). *The process of education.* Vintage Books.

Bruner, J. (1973). *The relevance of education.* W. W. Norton.

Bugental, J. F. T. (1964). The person who is the psychotherapist. *Journal of Consulting Psychology, 28*(3), 272–277. https://doi.org/10.1037/h0049013

Bugental, J. F. T. (1987). *The art of psychotherapy.* W. W. Norton.

Centers for Disease Control and Prevention. (2021) *Data and statistics about ADHD.* www.cdc.gov/ncbddd/adhd/data.html

Cepeda, L. M., & Davenport, D. S. (2006). Person-centered therapy and solution-focused brief therapy: An integration of present and future awareness. *Psychotherapy: Theory, Research, Practice, Training, 43*(1), 1–12.

Chambless, D. L., & Hollon, S. D. (1998). Defining empirically supported therapies. *Journal of Consulting and Clinical Psychology, 66*(1), 7–18. https://doi.org/10.1037/0022-006X.66.1.7

Combs, A. W. (1954). Counseling as a learning process. *Journal of Counseling Psychology, 1*(1), 31–36.

Cowman, S. E., Ferrari, J. R., & Liao-Troth, M. (2004). Mediating effects of social support on firefighters' sense of community and perceptions of care. *Journal of Community Psychology, 32*(2), 121–126.

Crenshaw, K. W., Gotanda, N., Peller, G., & Thomas, K. (1995). *Critical race theory: The key writings that formed a movement.* New Press.

Crethar, H. C., Rivera, E. T., & Nash, S. (2008). In search of common threads: Linking multicultural, feminist, and social justice counseling paradigms. *Journal of Counseling & Development, 86*(3), 269–278.

Crook, S. (2018). The women's liberation movement, activism and therapy at the grassroots, 1968–1985. *Women's History Review, 27*(7), 1152–1168.

Cuijpers, P., Driessen, E., Hollon, S. D., van Oppen, P., Barth, J., & Andersson, G. (2012). The efficacy of non-directive supportive therapy for adult depression: A meta-analysis. *Clinical Psychology Review, 32*(4), 280–291.

D'Andrea, M. (2000). Postmodernism, constructivism, and multiculturalism: Three forces reshaping and expanding our thoughts about counseling. *Journal of Mental Health Counseling, 22*(1), 1–16.

Dagirmanjian, S., Eron, J., & Lund, T. (2007). Narrative solutions: an integration of self and systems perspectives in motivating change. *Journal of Psychotherapy Integration, 17*(1), 70–92.

Davies, M. (1976). Systems theory and social work. In J. P. Beishon and G. Peters (Ed.), *Systems Behavior* (2nd ed., pp. 270–289). Harper & Row.

Davis, N. (1996). *Once upon a time … therapeutic stories that teach and heal.*

De Jong, P., & Berg, I. (2007). *Interviewing for solutions* (3rd ed.). Brooks/Cole.

De Shazer, S. (1985). *Keys to solution in brief therapy.* W. W. Norton.

Diller, J. V., & Moule, J. (2000). *Cultural competence: A primer for educators.* Thomson Wadsworth.

Dimaggio, G., Salvatore, G., Azzara, C., & Catania, D. (2003). Rewriting self-narratives: The therapeutic process. *Journal of Constructivist Psychology, 16*(2), 155–181.

Dubi, M., Powell, P., & Gentry, J. E. (2017). *Trauma, PTSD, grief & loss: The 10 core competencies for evidence-based treatment.* PESI Publishing & Media.

Dubois, A. L., Levers, L. L., & Esposito, C. P. (2012). Existential perspectives on the psychology of evil. In L. Levers (Ed.), *Trauma counseling* (pp. 264–279). Springer.

Duncan, B., Miller, S., Wamplod, B., & Hubble, M. (2010). *The heart and soul of change: Delivering what works in therapy* (2nd ed.). American Psychological Association.

EchoHawk, M. (2010). 7 suicides: The scourge of native American people. *Suicide and Life-Threatening Behavior, 27*(1), 60–67.

Ellenberger, H. (1970). The discovery of the unconscious: The history and evolution of dynamic psychiatry. Basic Books.

Elliott, R., Bohart, A. C., Watson, J. C., & Murphy, D. (2019). Empathy. In J. C. Norcross & M. J. Lambert (Eds.), *Psychotherapy relationships that work: Evidence-based therapist contributions* (pp. 245–287). Oxford University Press.

Ellis, A. (1974). Rational-emotive theory: Albert Ellis. In A. Burton (Ed.), *Operational theories of personality* (pp. 308–344). Brunner/Mazel.

Epston, D., & White, M. (1994). *Experience, contradiction, narrative & imagination: selected papers of David Epston & Michael White, 1989–1991*. Dulwich Centre Publications.

Erickson, M. H. (1954). Pseudo-orientation in time as a hypnotic procedure. *Journal of Clinical and Experimental Hypnosis, 2*, 261–283.

Farley, N. (2008). *Living in paradox: The theory and practice of contextual existentialism*. University Press of America.

Festinger, L. (1962). Cognitive dissonance. *Scientific American, 207*(4), 93–106.

Fisch, R., Weakland, J. H., & Segal, L. (1982). *The tactics of change: Doing therapy briefly*. Jossey-Bass.

Fisher, J. (2010). Brain to brain: The therapist as neurobiological regulator. *Psychotherapy Networker, 34*(1).

Fishman, D. B. (1999). *The case for pragmatic psychology*. New York University Press.

Foa, E. B., & Rothbaum, B. O. (1998). *Treating the trauma of rape: Cognitive-behavioral therapy for PTSD*. Guilford Press.

Fong, M. L. (1993). Teaching assessment and diagnosis within a DSM-III-R framework. *Counselor Education and Supervision, 32*(4), 276–286. https://doi.org/10.1002/j.1556-6978.1993.tb00255.x

Foucault, M. (1977). *Discipline and punish: The birth of the prison*. Pantheon Books.

Frank, J. D. (1987). Psychotherapy, rhetoric, and hermeneutics: Implications for practice and research. *Psychotherapy: Theory, Research, Practice, Training, 24*(3), 293–302.

Frank, J. D., & Frank, J. B. (1991). *Persuasion and healing: A comparative study of psychotherapy* (3rd ed.). Johns Hopkins University Press.

Frankl, V. (1968). *Man's search for meaning*. Washington Square Press. (Original work published 1949)

Freire, P. (1973). *Education for critical consciousness*. Bloomsbury.

Freire, P. (1990). *Pedagogy of the oppressed*. Continuum.

Freud, S. (1933). *New introductory lectures on psycho-analysis*. W. W. Norton.

Freud, S., & Breuer, J. (2004). *Studies in hysteria (N. Luckhurst, Trans.)*. Penguin Books.

Friedman, J., & Combs, G. (1996). *Narrative therapy: The social construction of preferred realities*. W. W. Norton.

Garner, C. M., Freeman, B. J., & Lee, L. (2016). *Assessment of student dispositions: The development and psychometric properties of the Professional Disposition Competence Assessment (PDCA)*. ACA Knowledge Center. https://www.counseling.org/knowledge-center/vistas/by-subject2/vistas-education-and-supervision/docs/default-source/vistas/article_5235f227f16116603abcacff0000bee5e7

Gay, R. (2016, July 11). On making Black lives matter. Marie Claire. https://www.marieclaire.com/culture/a21423/roxane-gay-philando-castile-alton-sterling/

Gentry, J. E., Baranowsky, A. B., & Rhoton, R. (2017). Trauma competency: An active ingredients approach to treating posttraumatic stress disorder. *Journal of Counseling & Development, 95*(3), 279–287.

Gilligan, C. (1982). *In a different voice*. Harvard University Press.

Gilligan, S. (1997). *The courage to heal: Principles and practices of self-relations psychotherapy*. W. W. Norton.

Gilligan, S. G., & Price, R. (Eds.). (1993). *Therapeutic conversations*. W. W. Norton.

Glasser, W. (1975). *Reality therapy: A new approach to psychiatry*. Harper & Row.

Goodyear, P. (2005). Educational design and networked learning: Patterns, pattern languages and design practice. *Australasian Journal of Educational Technology, 21*(1).

Gottman, J. M. (1995). *The analysis of change*. Psychology Press.

Greenberg, L., & Paivio, S. (1997). *Working with emotions in psychotherapy*. The Guilford Press.

Granello, D. H. (2010). Cognitive complexity among practicing counselors: How thinking changes experience. *Journal of Counseling & Development, 88*(1), 92–100.

Gunnar, M. R., & Vazquez, D. (2006). Stress neurobiology and developmental psychopathology. In D. Cicchetti & D. J. Cohen (Eds.), *Developmental psychopathology: Developmental neuroscience* (pp. 533–577). John Wiley & Sons.

Haase, L., Thom, N. L., Shukla, A., Davenport, P. W., Simmons, A. N., Stanley, E. A., Paulus, M. P., & Johnson, D. C. (2016). Mindfulness-based training attenuates insula response to an aversive interoceptive challenge. *Social Cognitive and Affective Neuroscience, 11*(1), 182–190.

Haley, J. (1987). *Problem-solving therapy* (2nd ed.). Jossey-Bass.

Hansen, J. T. (2007). Counseling without truth: Toward a neopragmatic foundation for counseling practice. *Journal of Counseling & Development, 85*(4), 423–430.

Hart, P., Wearing, A., & Headey, B. (1995). Police stress and well-being: Integrating personality, coping and daily work experiences. *Journal of Occupational and Organizational Psychology, 68*, 133–156.

Haslam, C., & Mallon, K. (2003). A preliminary investigation of post-traumatic stress symptoms among firefighters. *Work & Stress, 17*(3), 277–285.

Hays, P. (2012). *Connecting across cultures*. Sage.

Hays, P. (2016). *Addressing cultural complexities in practice: Assessment, diagnosis, and therapy*. American Psychological Association.

Heider, F. (1958). *The psychology of interpersonal relations*. John Wiley & Sons.

Herman, J. (1997). *Trauma and recovery; The aftermath of violence: From domestic abuse to political terror*. Basic Books.

Hinton, E. (2017). *From the war on poverty to the war on crime*. Harvard University Press.

Hobfoll, S. E., Jackson, A., Hobfoll, I., Pierce, C. A., & Young, S. (2002). The impact of communal-mastery versus self-mastery on emotional outcomes during stressful conditions: A prospective study of native American women. *American Journal of Community Psychology, 30*, 853–871.

Hoffman, L. (1981). *Foundations of family therapy*. Basic Books.

Hoffman, L., Stewart, S., Warren, D., & Meek, L. (2009). Toward a sustainable myth of self: An existential response to the postmodern condition. *Journal of Humanistic Psychology, 49*(2), 135–173.

Hubble, M. A., Duncan, B., & Miller, S. (1999). *The heart and soul of change: What works in therapy*. American Psychological Association.

Hubble, M. A., & Miller, S. D. (2004). The client: Psychotherapy's missing link for promoting a positive psychology. In P. A. Linley & S. Joseph (Eds.), *Positive psychology in practice* (pp. 335–353). John Wiley & Sons.

Iwasaki, M. (2005). Mental health and counseling in Japan: A path toward societal transformation. *Journal of Mental Health Counseling, 27*(2), 129–141.

Jones, S. R., & McEwen, M. K. (2000). A conceptual model of multiple dimensions of Identity. *Journal of College Student Development, 41*(4), 405–414.

Jones-Smith, E. (2019). *Culturally diverse counseling: Theory and practice*. Sage.

Jordan, J. V., Kaplan, A. G., Miller, J. B., Stiver, I. P., Surrey, J. L., & Stone Center for Developmental Services and Studies. (1991). *Women's growth in connection: Writings from the stone center*. Guilford Press.

Joseph, D. L., & Newman, D. A. (2010). Emotional intelligence: An integrative meta-analysis and cascading model. *Journal of Applied Psychology, 95*(1), 54–78.

Katz, M. M., & Lyerly, S. B. (1963). Methods for measuring adjustment and social behavior in the community: Rationale, description, discriminative validity, and scale development. *Psychological Reports, 13*(2), 503–535.

Kwan, V. S. Y., Bond, M. H., & Singelis, T. M. (1997). Pancultural explanations for life satisfaction: Adding relationship harmony to self-esteem. *Journal of Personality and Social Psychology, 73*(5), 1038–1051.

Kierkegaard, S. (1954). *Fear and trembling and the sickness unto death*. Princeton University Press.

Kitayama, S., & Markus, H. R. (1999). Yin and Yang of the Japanese self: The cultural psychology of personality coherence. In D. Cervone & Y. Shoda (Eds.), *The coherence of personality: Social-cognitive bases of consistency, variability, and organization* (pp. 242–302). Guilford Press.

Koffka, K. (1935). *Principles of gestalt psychology*. Routledge.

Kohlberg, L., & Mayer, R. (1972). Development as the aim of education: The Dewey view. *Harvard Educational Review, 42*, 449–496.

Kohler, W. (1925). *The mentality of apes*. Harcourt, Brace & Company.

Kondo, D. K. (1990). *Crafting selves: Power, gender, and discourses of identity in a Japanese workplace.* The University of Chicago Press.

Kuhn, T. S. (1970). *The structure of scientific revolutions* (2nd ed.). University of Chicago Press.

Lambert, M. J. (1992). Psychotherapy outcome research: Implications for integrative and eclectical therapists. In J. C. Norcross & M. R. Goldfried (Eds.), *Handbook of psychotherapy integration* (pp. 94–129). Basic Books.

Lanzoni, S. M. (2018). *Empathy: A history.* Yale University Press.

Lawrence, C., Foster, V. A., & Tieso, C. L. (2015). Creating creative clinicians: Incorporating creativity into counselor education. *Journal of Creativity in Mental Health, 10*(2), 166–180.

Lefevor, G. T., Boyd-Rogers, C. C., Sprague, B. M., & Janis, R. A. (2019). Health disparities between genderqueer, transgender, and cisgender individuals: An extension of minority stress theory. *Journal of Counseling Psychology, 66*(4), 385–395.

Linehan, M. M. (1993). *Cognitive-behavioral treatment of borderline personality disorder.* Guilford Press.

Lipchik, E. (2011). *Beyond technique in solution-focused therapy: Working with emotions and the therapeutic relationship.* Guilford Publications.

Madanes, C. (1981). *Strategic family therapy.* Jossey-Bass.

Maddux, J. E. (2002). Self-efficacy: The power of believing you can. In C. R. Snyder & S. J. Lopez (Eds.), *Handbook of positive psychology* (pp. 277–287). Oxford University Press.

Mainardi, P. (1970). *The politics of housework.* New England Free Press.

Maslow, A. H. (1943). A theory of human motivation. *Psychological Review, 50*(4), 370–396.

Maslow, A. H. (1962). Notes on being-psychology. *Journal of Humanistic Psychology, 2*(2), 47–71.

Maturana, H. R., & Varela, F. J. (1987). *The tree of knowledge: The biological roots of human understanding.* Shambhala.

May, R. (1950). *The meaning of anxiety.* Martino Fine Books.

May, R. (1982). The problem with evil: An open letter to Carl Rogers. *Journal of Humanist Psychology 22*(3), 10–21.

McGilchrist, I. (2009). *Master & his emissary: The divided brain and the making of the western world.* Yale University Press.

McNamee, S. J., & Miller, R. K. (2004). *The meritocracy myth.* Rowman & Littlefield.

Meichenbaum, D. (1985). *Stress inoculation training.* Pergamon Press.

Menakem, R. (2017). *My grandmother's hands: Racialized trauma and the pathway to mending our hearts and bodies.* Central Recovery Press.

Mesut, C., Kose, S., Ebrinc, S., Yigit, S., Elhai, J. D., & Basoglu, C. (2005). Identification and posttraumatic stress disorder symptoms in rescue workers in the Marmara, Turkey earthquake. *Journal of Traumatic Stress, 18*(5), 485–489.

Meyer, I. H. (2003). Prejudice, social stress, and mental health in lesbian, gay and bisexual populations: Conceptual issues and research evidence. *Psychological Bulletin, 129*(5), 674–697.

Mezirow, J. (1991). *Transformative dimensions of adult learning.* Jossey-Bass.

Mezirow, J. (1994). Understanding transformation theory. *Adult Education Quarterly, 44*(4), 222–232.

Miller, D. (2001). The poverty of morality. *Journal of Consumer Culture, 1*(2), 225–243.

Miller, W. R., & Rollnick, S. (2002). *Motivational interviewing.* Guilford.

Minuchin, S. (1974). *Families and family therapy.* Harvard University Press.

Mousavi, S., & Gigerenzer, G. (2014). Risk, uncertainty, and heuristics. *Journal of Business Research, 67*(8), 1671–1678.

Murphy, G., & Kovach, J. (1972). *Historical introduction to modern psychology.* Harcourt Brace Jovanovich.

Nehls, N. (1998). Borderline personality disorder: Gender stereotypes, stigma, and limited system of care. *Issues in Mental Health Nursing, 19*(2), 97–112.

Nichols, M. P., & Schwartz, R. C. (1998). *Family therapy: Concepts and methods* (4th ed.). Allyn and Bacon.

Norcross, J. C. (Ed.). (2002). *Psychotherapy relationships that work: Therapist contributions and responsiveness to patients.* Oxford University Press.

Norcross, J., & Drewes, A. (2009). Self-care for child therapists: Leaving it at the office. In A. Drewes (Ed.), *Blending play therapy with cognitive behavioral therapy: Evidence-based and other effective treatments and techniques* (473–493). Wiley & Sons.

Norcross, J. C., & Lambert, M. J. (2011). Evidence-based therapy relationships. In J. C. Norcross (Ed.), *Psychotherapy relationships that work: Evidence-based responsiveness* (pp. 3–21). Oxford University Press.

Norcross, J. C., & Lambert, M. J. (2018). Psychotherapy relationships that work. *Psychotherapy, 55*(4), 303–315.

Norcross, J., & Lambert, M. (2019). *Psychotherapy relationships that work: Vol. 1. Evidence-based therapist contributions* (3rd ed.). Oxford University Press.

Norcross, J., & Wampold, B. (2019). *Psychotherapy relationships that work: Vol. 2. Evidence-based therapist responsiveness* (3rd ed.). Oxford University Press.

O'Hanlon, B. (1987). *Taproots: Underlying principles of Milton Erickson's therapy and hypnosis.* W. W. Norton.

Pacella, B. L. (1984). Review of the book *Paradox and Counterparadox,* by M. Selvini Palazzoli, G. Cecchin, G. Prata, and L. Boscolo. *Journal of the American Psychoanalytic Association, 32*(3), 677–680.

Palazzoli, M. S., & Pomerans, A. J. (1996). *Self-starvation: from individual to family therapy in the treatment of anorexia nervosa.* J. Aronson.

Paton, D. (1994). Disaster relief work: An assessment of training effectiveness. *Journal of Traumatic Stress, 7*(2), 275–288.

Patterson, A. H. (1974). Hostility catharsis: A naturalistic quasi-experiment. *Proceedings of the Division of Personality and Society Psychology, 1*(1), 195–197.

Pavlov, I. P. (1928). *Lectures on conditioned reflexes: Twenty-five years of objective study of the higher nervous activity (behavior) of animals* (W. H. Gantt, Trans.). Liverwright Publishing Corporation.

Pennebaker, J.W., Kiecolt-Glaser, J., & Glaser, R. (1988). Disclosure of traumas and immune function: Health implications for psychotherapy. *Journal of Consulting and Clinical Psychology, 56,* 239–245.

Perls, F. (1969). *Gestalt therapy verbatim.* Real People Press.

Piaget, J. (1954). *The construction of reality in the child.* Basic Books.

Piaget, J. (1970). *Structuralism.* Basic Books.

Piaget, J. (1973). *The child and reality: Problems of genetic psychology* (A Rosin, Trans.). Grossman Publishers.

Rank, O. (1989). *Art and artist. Creative urge and personality development.* W. W. Norton. (Original work published 1932)

Rank, O. (2011). *Beyond psychology.* Dover Publications. (Original work published 1941)

Rapp, C. A. (1998). *The strengths model: Case management with people suffering from severe and persistent mental illness.* Oxford University Press.

Rashid, T., & Ostermann, R. F. (2009). Strength-based assessment in clinical practice. *Journal of Clinical Psychology, 65*(5), 488.

Ratts, J. M., Singh, A. A., Nassar-McMillan, S., Butler, K. S., & McCullough, J. R. (2015). *Multicultural and social justice competencies.* Association for Multicultural Counseling and Development Executive Council.

Regehr, C., Goldberg, G., & Hughes, J. (2002). Exposure to human tragedy, empathy, and trauma in ambulance paramedics. *American Journal of Orthopsychiatry, 72*(4), 505–513.

Rogers, C. R. (1942). *Counseling and psychotherapy: Newer concepts in practice.* (L. Carmichael, Ed.). Houghton Mifflin.

Rogers, C. R. (1951). *Client-centered therapy: Its current practice, implications, and theory.* Houghton Mifflin.

Rogers, C. R. (1957). The necessary and sufficient conditions of therapeutic personality change. *Journal of Consulting Psychology, 21*(2), 95–103.

Rogers, C. R. (1961). *On becoming a person: A psychotherapists view of psychotherapy.* Houghton Mifflin.

Rogers, C. R. (1977). *Carl Rogers on personal power.* Delacorte.

Rogers, C. R. (1981). The foundations of the person-centered approach. *Dialectics and Humanism*, *8*(1), 5–16.

Rogers, C. R. (1986). Carl Rogers on the development of the person-centered approach. *Person-Centered Review*, *1*(3), 257–259.

Rogers, C. R. (1995). What understanding and acceptance mean to me. *Journal of Humanistic Psychology*, *35*(4).

Rogers, C. R., Stevens, B., Gendlin, E. T., Shlien, J. M., & Van Dusen, W. (1967). *Person to person: The problem of being human: A new trend in psychology*. Real People Press.

Rosenberger, N. R. (1992). The process of discourse: Usages of a Japanese medical term. *Social Science & Medicine*, *35*(3), 237–247.

Ross, L. (1977). The intuitive psychologist and his shortcomings: Distortions in the attribution process. *Advances in Experimental Social Psychology*, *10*, 173–220.

Rossi, P. H. (1980). *Why families move* (2nd ed.). Sage Publications.

Rotter, J. B. (1954). *Social learning and clinical psychology*. Prentice Hall.

Russell, B. (1908). Mathematical logic as based on the theory of types. *American Journal of Mathematics*, *30*, 222–262.

Saleebey, D. (2001). *Human behavior and social environments: A biopsychosocial approach*. Columbia University Press.

Santamaria, M. C. (1990). Couples therapy: Analysis of a "praxis" with a Freirian perspective. *Family Process*, *29*(2), 119–129.

Satir, V. (1984). *Satir step by step: A guide to creating change in families*. Science and Behavior Books.

Satir, V. (1998). *The new people-making*. Science and Behavior Books.

Scheel, M. J., Berman, M., Friedlander, M. L., Conoley C. W., Duan, C., Whiston, S. C. (2011). Whatever happened to counseling in counseling Psychology? *The Counseling Psychologist*, *39*(5), 673–692.

Schon, D. A. (1987). *Educating the reflective practitioner: Toward a new design for teaching and learning in the professions*. Jossey-Bass.

Schore, A. (2019). *The development of the unconsciousness mind*. W. W. Norton.

Schore, A. (2003). *Affect regulation and the repair of the self*. W. W. Norton.

Seligman, M. (2002). Positive psychology, positive prevention, and positive therapy. In C. R. Snyder & S. J. Lopez (Eds.), *Handbook of positive psychology* (pp. 3–9). Oxford University Press.

Seligman, M. E., & Maier, S. F. (1967). Failure to escape traumatic shock. *Journal of Experimental Psychology*, *74*(1), 1–9.

Selman, R. L. (1980). *The growth of interpersonal understanding*. Academic Press.

Selvini Palazzoli, M. (1986). *Self-starvation: From individual to family therapy in the treatment of anorexia nervosa*. Jason Aronson.

Sexton, G. (2007). Relationships as the key to attracting and keeping people. *Australian Journal of Career Development*, *16*(1), 66–69. https://doi.org/10.1177/103841620701600112

Shapiro, F., & Forrest, M. S. (1997). *EMDR: The breakthrough therapy for overcoming anxiety, stress, and trauma*. Basic Books .

Sharf, R. S. (1996). *Theories of psychotherapy and counseling: Concepts and cases*. Brooks/Cole Pub.

Simard, S. (2021). *Finding the mother tree: Discovering the wisdom of the forest*. Knopf.

Skinner, B. F. (1953). *Science and human behavior*. The Macmillan Company.

Stanley, S. (2016). *Relational and body-centered practices for healing trauma: Lifting the burdens of the past*. Routledge.

Surrey, J. L. (1991). The "self in relation": A theory of women's development. In J. V. Jordan, A. G. Kaplan, J. Baker-Miller, I. P. Stiver, & J. L. Surrey (Eds.), *Women's growth in connection: Writings from the stone center* (pp. 51–66). Guildford Press.

Tajfel, H. (1969). Cognitive aspects of prejudice. *Journal of Biosocial Science*, *1*(Suppl. 1), 173–191.

Taylor, J. M., Gilligan, C., & Sullivan, A. M. (1995). *Between voice and silence: Women and girls, race and relationship.* Harvard University Press.

Teyber, E., & McClure, F. H. (2011). *Interpersonal process in therapy: An integrative model* (6th ed.). Cengage Learning.

The Trevor Project. (2021, March 11). *Estimates of how often LGBTQ youth attempt suicide in the U.S.* https://www.thetrevorproject.org/research-briefs/estimate-of-how-often-lgbtq-youth-attempt-suicide-in-the-u-s/

Thomas, L. (2007). The therapist as a moderator and mediator in successful therapeutic change. *Journal of Family Therapy, 29*(2), 104–108.

Truax, C. B., & Carkhuff, R. R. (1967). *Toward effective counseling and psychotherapy: Training and practice.* Aldine Publishing Co.

Tugade, M. M., & Fredrickson, B. L. (2004). Resilient individuals use positive emotions to bounce back from negative emotional experiences. *Journal of Personality and Social Psychology, 86*(2), 320–333.

Unger, M. (2013). Resilience, trauma, context, and culture. *Trauma Violence & Abuse, 14*(3), 255–266.

van der Kolk, B., Weisaeth, L., & van der Hart, O. (1996). History of trauma in psychiatry. In B. van der Kolk, A. McFarlane, & L. Weisaeth, (Eds.), *Traumatic stress: The effects of overwhelming experience on mind, body, and society* (pp. 47–74). The Guilford Press.

van der Kolk, B. A. (2014). *The body keeps the score: Brain, mind, and body in the healing of trauma.* Penguin Books.

Vera E. M., & Speight S. L. (2003). Multicultural competence, social justice, and counseling psychology: Expanding our roles. *The Counseling Psychologist, 31*(3), 253–272.

Vygotsky, L. (1978). *Interaction between learning and development.* In V. Cole, S. John-Steiner, & E. Souberman (Eds.), *Mind and society: The development of higher psychological processes* (pp. 79–91). Harvard University Press.

Wampold, B. E. (2001). *The great psychotherapy debate: Models, methods, and findings.* Lawrence Erlbaum.

Ward, C., & House, R. (1998). Counseling supervision: A reflective model. *Counselor Education and Supervision, 38*(1), 23–33.

Ward, C., & Reuter, T. (2011). *Strength centered counseling: Integrating postmodern approaches and skills with practice.* Sage.

Waters, A., & Asbill, L. (2013). *Reflections on cultural humility.* American Psychological Association.

Watson, J. B. (1913). Psychology as the behaviorist views it. *Psychological Review, 20*(2), 158–177.

Watzlawick, P., Beavin, J. H., & Jackson, D. (1967). *Programatics of human communication: A study of interactional patterns, pathologies, and paradoxes.* Norton.

Watzlawick, P., Weakland, J. H., & Fisch, R. (1974). *Change: Principles of problem formation and problem resolution.* W. W. Norton.

Weakland, J. H., Fisch, R., Watzlawick, P., & Bodin, A. M. (1974). Brief therapy: Focused problem resolution. *Family Process, 13*(2), 141–168.

Wertheimer, M. (1923). Laws of organization in perceptual forms. *Psycologische Forschung, 4*, 301–350.

Wegner, D. M., & Bargh, J. A. (1998). Control and automaticity in social life. In D. T. Gilbert, S. T. Fiske, & G. Lindzey (Eds.), *The handbook of social psychology* (pp. 446–496). McGraw-Hill.

Werner, E. E., & Smith, R. S. (1992). *Overcoming the odds: High risk children from birth to adulthood.* Cornell University Press.

Wheeler, J. A., & Zurek, W. H. (1984). *Quantum theory and measurement.* Princeton University Press

White, M. (2007). *Maps of narrative practice.* W. W. Norton.

White, M., & Epston, D. (1990). *Narrative means to therapeutic ends.* W. W. Norton.

Whitehead, A. N. & Russell, B. (1962). *Principia Mathmatica to 56.* Cambridge University Press. (Original work published 1908)

Yalom, I. (1980). *Existential psychotherapy.* Basic Books.

Yalom, I. (2005). *The Schopenhauer cure.* Harper-Collins.

Yalom, I. (2008). Staring into the sun: Overcoming the terror of death. *The Humanistic Psychologist. 36*(3-4), 283–297.

Index

CPSIA information can be obtained
at www.ICGtesting.com
Printed in the USA
LVHW061115200422
716652LV00001B/15